Think Like a Lawyer

Act Like an Entrepreneur

STEPHEN E. SECKLER

ABA
AMERICAN BAR ASSOCIATION
Solo, Small Firm and General Practice Division

Cover design by Jill Tedhams/ABA Design

Library of Congress Cataloging-in-Publication Data

Names: Seckler, Stephen E., author.
Title: Think like a lawyer, act like an entrepreneur section / Stephen E. Seckler.
Description: First edition. | Chicago : American Bar Association, 2025. | Includes index. | Summary: "Many books on legal and marketing focus on mindset. Here, I focus on changing behavior-not waiting until you feel ready, but taking small, actionable steps. You don't need to think like an entrepreneur to act like one. As you implement these actions, your mindset will evolve, but the focus here is to help you take concrete steps toward marketing success. My own journey began in the late 1980s, during the rise of legal marketing. After law school, I worked in continuing legal education, where I learned firsthand about the value of relationship building in legal marketing. Over time, I took the entrepreneurial leap and launched my own business, transitioning to legal recruiting and coaching. This journey taught me that building a practice involves embracing discomfort, taking action, and stepping away from traditional legal thinking. I've come to see marketing as a virtuous activity and a way to serve others. This book is a culmination of what I've been teaching lawyers since the 1990s: building a practice means cultivating relationships and stepping out of your comfort zone. If you want to build your practice but dislike marketing, this book is for you. Not everyone needs to be a superstar rainmaker. By taking small steps, you can generate the clients you want and have a fulfilling legal career"-- Provided by publisher.
Identifiers: LCCN 2024057754 | ISBN 9781639056026 (paperback) | ISBN 9781639056033 (epub)
Subjects: LCSH: Lawyers--United States. | Practice of law--Economic aspects--United States. | Businesspeople--United States.
Classification: LCC KF315 .S43 2025 | DDC 340.023/73--dc23/eng/20241203
LC record available at https://lccn.loc.gov/2024057754

Printed in the United States of America.

29 28 27 26 25 5 4 3 2

Discounts are available for books ordered in bulk. Special consideration is given to state bars, CLE programs, and other bar-related organizations. Inquire at Book Publishing, ABA Publishing, American Bar Association, 321 N. Clark Street, Chicago, Illinois 60654-7598.

www.shopABA.org

Working with Steve as our firm's rainmaking coach was a great experience. Steve's guidance not only helped us set clear objectives but also provided the necessary tools to achieve them. *Think Like a Lawyer, Act Like an Entrepreneur* brings together the many valuable insights he shared with us. It is a field guide for any lawyer who is skeptical about marketing. Lawyers who are uncomfortable with selling should read this book.

—Domenic Romano, Managing Partner, Romano Law PLLC

Hands down the best guide to business development for the 21st century lawyer. A comprehensive playbook packed with simple, actionable advice, real-world examples, and checklists (pure gold) that will resonate even with the most uber-analytical, risk-averse attorney. Seckler offers clear, refreshingly practical strategies that are as useful to lawyers leery of "salesy" marketing activities as to more outgoing practitioners. He also makes a compelling case for coaching.

—Elizabeth H. Munnell, business development coach, ehmunnell.com

Lawyers need to think like lawyers when practicing law; for everything else, they need to pay attention to and implement the tips Steve offers throughout this book. I've known Steve for many years and witnessed the evolution of his marketing skills. I can attest that he was not a born salesman and has slid beautifully into the sales world by generating work through helpfulness, referrals, and authentic advice. His book captures pretty much everything you need to know to build a practice, even if you don't agree with everything. Every lawyer will benefit from what this book teaches.

—Jim Durham, Jim Durham Consulting

Steve's years of experience and successes shine through in this book. Lawyers will learn to apply practical, creative, and user-friendly strategies that will grow their practices.

—Merry Neitlich, Founder and Managing Partner, EM Consulting

While there are countless excellent books for lawyers (and I've written a few myself), this one stands out as the "fish out of water" guide to growth for attorneys. In this refreshingly honest and down-to-earth book, Steve shares personal life lessons and hard-earned wisdom to help lawyers avoid the pitfalls he encountered along the way. Steve's candid insights make this book not just relatable but invaluable for any lawyer striving to build their book of business. If you're uncomfortable with "selling legal services," I wholeheartedly recommend this book.

—Steve Fretzin, President, BE THAT LAWYER with FRETZIN

An essential field guide for attorneys attempting to get out of their own heads and unleash the business marketing dynamo within. It's true that lawyers are trained to be risk-averse. Of course, that's not so great a quality to have as an entrepreneur; building a business, acquiring clients—it's all fraught with risk and coded for regular failures. In his book, Steve relays how he overcame these built-in barriers to make himself a successful entrepreneur—the same way you can.

—Jared D. Correia, CEO, Red Cave Law Firm Consulting

Dedicated with love to my late father, Bernie Seckler, who taught me the values of learning, integrity, hard work, and puns. And to my wife, Jenny Gamson, who has supported my long journey from thinking like a lawyer to acting like a successful entrepreneur.

Contents

Acknowledgments

It is difficult to pinpoint the individuals who have had the most impact on my career and who have had the greatest influence on my thinking. There are so many, and I continue to meet more all of the time. Some are people who I know well, and others are thought leaders who I have never met. Some are people who have provided me with the encouragement I needed to finally write a book. This is only a partial list (with apologies to the many others who I have not mentioned):

- Numerous thought leaders and podcast hosts including Daniel Kahneman (the father of behavioral economics), Shankar Vedantam (*Hidden Brain* podcast), Laurie Santos (professor at Yale and host of *The Happiness Lab* podcast), Adam Grant (professor at the Wharton School of the University of Pennsylvania and author of *Give and Take*), Carol Dweck (*Mindset: The New Psychology of Success*), Richard Boyatzis (*Helping People Change*), Neil Rackham (*SPIN Selling*), and Martin Seligman (the father of positive psychology)
- Jim Durham and Harry Keshet who taught me over 30 years ago that marketing professional services is about *service* and not about *selling.*
- Many member of the ProVisors business network, including Steve Fretzin (*Be That Lawyer*) and Gary Johnson, who have really elevated my marketing skills); Beth Masterman (whose support and mentoring have made me a much better coach); Chris Murphy (*Call me if you or a loved one are in the back of an ambulance or the back of a hearse*), and Bob Donahoe, who both welcomed me with open arms into the ProVisors community and taught me the value of choosing your lane; Jennifer Taddeo (*I bring death and taxes to life*), who encouraged me to join and taught me how to benefit from the platform; Saja Raoof (*Border wall destroyer*, introvert, and lover of hummus), who taught me the art of authenticity; and many other members who have taught me the value of being a *go giver*.

- Amy Levine for her belief in me when I was struggling as a recruiter and who not only understands how lawyers think but understands what it is like to grow up in New York with neurotic Jewish parents.
- All my coaching clients who put their faith in me to help them find more success and career satisfaction in—or outside—of law, and who inspire me with *their* successes.
- Rob Salkin, Emily Roy, and Lorraine Murray of the American Bar Association for their support and encouragement.
- Jared Correia, who inspired me to launch the *Counsel to Counsel Podcast* and who shares my love of stupid dad jokes, and Stefanie Marrone, who writes extensively about how to leverage LinkedIn in the legal profession and who inspires me to be generous with my own thought leadership.
- Most importantly, Dr. Larry Richard, whose extensive research and thinking on lawyer personalities has had tremendous influence on my own understanding of the beliefs we hold as attorneys and the behaviors we display that undermine our success. Larry's work is the inspiration for this book. His footprint and thought leadership are felt on many of these pages.

Author Bio

Stephen E. Seckler, Esq., is president of Seckler Attorney Coaching in Newton, Massachusetts. He is an award-winning coach who helps lawyers achieve greater career satisfaction. For over 25 years, he has guided hundreds of attorneys nationwide, coaching them on business development, career transitions, and leadership.

A former recruiter and CLE professional, Steve joined the ABA Career Center Board in 2023 and has hosted the *Counsel to Counsel* podcast since 2018. His blog was twice named to the *ABA Journal's Blawg 100*, and he contributes regularly to ABA publications.

Steve frequently speaks for bar associations and guests on legal podcasts. He is a member of the Mindfulness in Law Society and the ProVisors business network. Since 2021, he has been ranked a top coach in the *Massachusetts Lawyers Weekly Reader Rankings Awards*.

Outside work, he enjoys behavioral economics, parody, squash, and choral singing. He is a proud father of three, including a law student graduating in 2025.

Introduction: Birth of a Salesman

I decided to write this book because I think like a lawyer. I'm a natural skeptic. I tend to overanalyze. I often see risk before opportunity. I'm a worrier. If you are reading these pages, perhaps you have similar wiring.

Over the past three decades, I've learned to take off my legal hat and pursue opportunities that advance my goals. This transformation wasn't about changing how I think (although my thinking did change). It was about changing my behavior. I hope this book helps you make a similar shift.

Thinking Like a Lawyer Has Value, but It Can Also Limit You

Thinking like a lawyer is not inherently bad; the world needs lawyers to manage risk. Your clients hire you to protect them from liability. But to build a practice, you must embrace calculated risks. This shift from skepticism to action will enhance both your career satisfaction and your success.

For years, I struggled with my natural inclination toward caution and my distaste of self-promotion. While my default thinking hasn't drastically changed, modifying my actions has made all the difference. I've coached hundreds of attorneys on how to move beyond their risk-averse tendencies, and this book is about doing just that.

This Book Is About Changing Behavior

Many books on legal and marketing[1] focus on mindset. Here, I focus on changing behavior—not waiting until you feel ready, but taking small, actionable steps

[1] I am using the word *marketing* here to mean both marketing (positioning and reputation-building activities) and business development (relationship-building activities and sales). I will use that shorthand periodically throughout this book.

now. You don't need to think like an entrepreneur to act like one. As you implement these actions, your mindset will evolve, but the focus here is to help you take concrete steps toward marketing success.

My own journey began in the late 1980s, during the rise of legal marketing. After law school, I worked in continuing legal education (CLE), where I learned firsthand about the value of relationship building in legal marketing. Over time, I took the entrepreneurial leap and launched my own business, transitioning to legal recruiting and coaching. This journey taught me that building a practice involves embracing discomfort, taking action, and stepping away from traditional legal thinking.

I've come to see marketing as a virtuous activity and a way to serve others. This book is a culmination of what I've been teaching lawyers since the 1990s: building a practice means cultivating relationships and stepping out of your comfort zone.

If you want to build your practice but dislike marketing, this book is for you. Not everyone needs to be a superstar rainmaker. By taking small steps, you can generate the clients you want and have a fulfilling legal career.

There are only three prerequisites: you have to like people (I thank Frank Rudewicz for that insight), you are willing to try out a few new ways of doing things, and you are willing to treat people the way *they* want to be treated (i.e., follow the "Platinum Rule").[2] The only thing standing between you and success is action.

Here is an overview of what follows. While the book is written with the intention that you might read it from cover to cover, many of the chapters do stand on their own, and I have included a number of checklists that I hope you will find useful regardless of how much of the book you read.

In Part 1, I set the stage by talking about the mindset we bring to the practice of law and provide some preliminary thoughts on what it takes to build a practice.

In Part 2, I discuss the importance of active listening in selling professional services and why that is the key skill to master.

In Part 3, I share some of my conventional and unconventional marketing advice, which has appeared in many of my American Bar Association (ABA) columns, blog posts, and LinkedIn posts.

In Part 4, I talk about thinking like a venture capitalist and offer miscellaneous other thoughts to help you in your marketing journey. I end with a discussion of how coaching can help you bridge the gap between knowing and doing.

---

[2] The Golden Rule advises treating others as you would like to be treated, while the Platinum Rule suggests treating others as they would like to be treated, focusing more on understanding and respecting individual preferences.

PART 1

Mindset and Getting Started

CHAPTER 1

Think Like a Lawyer, but Stop Acting Like One

There is something I've been pondering since I passed the bar in the late 1980s—do people who think like lawyers gravitate toward law school, or does going to law school and practicing law change the way you think?[1]

In my opinion, the answer is, a little of both. Law is a conservative profession, and it tends to attract people who are skeptical and risk averse (accounting and medicine are similar). In contrast, people who choose a career in business are thinking more about opportunity than about risk. At the same time, what do lawyers do all day long? They help clients figure out what might go wrong and advise them on how to manage those risks. If you are already predisposed to avoiding risk, practicing law reinforces your risk aversion.

Helping clients effectively manage risk is what makes for a great lawyer. Being skeptical is a way to tease out how significant the risks are for your client. Your job is to protect your clients from unnecessary risk.

The problem is that the things that make you a great lawyer are things that can get in the way when you are trying to build your practice or navigate your career.

Of course, the world does need lawyers. We play a valuable role in society. If the world were made only of entrepreneurs, it would be a much more dangerous place. But if the world were made only of lawyers, nothing would ever get accomplished.

[1] Much of the background for this chapter (and for this book as a whole) is based on the work of Dr. Larry Richard, who has done more research on lawyer personalities than anyone. To read more about Dr. Richard and his work, visit https://www.lawyerbrain.com/.

PRACTICING LAW REQUIRES LINEAR THINKING, BUT BUILDING A PRACTICE IS NOT A LINEAR PROCESS

In the practice of law, there is an end point in your work. You are trying to get a deal done, file a motion, settle a case, or help a client comply with statutes and regulations. You are looking to protect your clients from liability. Your linear and structured thinking helps you solve the client's problem. As a lawyer, you help clients understand and navigate the legal system, ensuring that their rights are protected, and their interests are advanced. Whether you are dealing with disputes, transactions, compliance, or planning, you are helping clients achieve their legal objectives and resolve their legal issues. A lot of your work is limited in duration. There is a beginning, a middle, and an end and there is often a recognized way of getting to that end point. As lawyers, we are good at creating the structure we need to deliver our services. We tend to be organized and like to follow logical steps and procedures.

Growing a law practice is a very different endeavor. It can take time to build your reputation in a niche. It can take years for some relationships to bear fruit. There is no starting point and there is no end point. And the path to success in marketing is anything but linear.

Practicing law requires structured thinking. Generating work requires flexibility.

Ultimately, work will come when you build the right relationships with the "right" potential clients and referral sources. When that will happen and how it will occur is unpredictable. My own recent experience illustrates this point.

In 2021, I got involved in the Senior Lawyers Division (SLD) of the ABA. I had started coaching senior attorneys on next-stage career transitions, and the SLD seemed like a good place for me to volunteer my time. As it turns out, Emily Roy, the ABA staff who oversees the division, is also responsible for the ABA Career Center. Eventually, she invited me to sit on the Career Center Board, which tends to serve a much younger demographic of the bar.

Being involved on the board led to my participation in the first real, live conferences I had been to since before the pandemic. And as I write about in chapter 9, attending one of those conferences led to a great introduction that has turned into a significant piece of coaching work for me. It was serendipity. But that serendipity would not have occurred without action.

IN DEVELOPING A NICHE, KEEP AN OPEN MIND

When you are new to the practice of law, you are trying to figure out where you want to focus your energy. Until you enter the profession, it is hard to know what type of work will resonate with you and what types of clients you want to work with. Also, as a junior associate, you may not have much choice about the work you are assigned.

In the early years, it is important to keep an open mind and pay attention to the work you *do* like and to the clients you like to serve. The more you gravitate toward the things you enjoy and the people you like, the greater the chance that you will be energized to find more of that work. Developing a niche requires keeping an open mind (possibly for many years). As lawyers, we tend to prefer closure, hoping to solve the problem and get to the end. In developing a niche, it is important to be more flexible.

Similarly, relationship building, which is the cornerstone of business development for all professional services, requires a lot of flexibility. You can create structure in your life that ensures that you are interacting with potential clients and referral sources—join a bar association committee, get active in a trade association, volunteer for a nonprofit cause you care about, coach youth sports, give presentations to community groups, etc. But the relationships you build will probably not come from structured interactions. Relationships grow more organically. You get to know people when you meet for coffee, when you invite them to a baseball game, when you get involved in a nonprofit cause you both care about, when you work together on a political campaign, or when you talk to other parents at back-to-school night.

One of my best clients is a managing partner I met 20 years ago through a philanthropic organization. We were on a panel together, and over the years, we met for coffee periodically. We would talk shop, but we also spoke about many other things—family, the organization we both supported, etc. Eventually, I began to do some recruiting for his firm, and, ultimately, I ended up working with him on his leadership skills.

In developing a niche, the end point is not obvious. And even when you figure out the end point, you will always be tweaking it as the legal landscape changes. The same is true for the relationships that you believe will lead to paying work.

So, be organized and structured when you are acting as a lawyer but be flexible when you are trying to build a practice.

ANALYTICAL THINKING MAKES YOU A BETTER LAWYER, BUT IT CAN INTERFERE WITH BUILDING TRUSTED RELATIONSHIPS

If you show up in the emergency room with nausea and extreme dizziness, you want a doctor who will figure out the root cause of your symptoms, not a doctor who shares your taste in music and who compliments you on your shirt (although it's nice if she does). When your client thinks someone is violating his trademark, he doesn't want to know where you spent your summer vacation (although that might come up in the conversation, and it could become a source of connection); he wants you to stop the financial "bleeding" and get an injunction.

Like doctors in the emergency room, lawyers who place greater emphasis on facts, objective data, and logic can see problems more clearly in a way that is helpful to their clients. Good analysis is good lawyering.

On the other hand, if you want to cultivate your business prospects for future business, that analytical thinking can get in the way of forming a genuine personal connection. The foundation of most trusted relationships is not a detached, data-driven exchange of information.

Imagine you are talking to the CEO of a software company who you were introduced to by an accountant you know. You are having coffee and trying to learn more about the business and perhaps learn more about the CEO. You don't know a lot about the CEO other than what you've read in his bio. You know a little more about the company because they are public, and you've looked at their public filings.

Early in the conversation, the CEO starts talking about a startup business that is in a similar space. The founder of the startup left the CEO's company with several key employees and is now competing directly.

While you may be tempted to start discussing the intricacies of noncompetes and offer up some case law analysis, this may be premature. This approach might overwhelm him, especially if he has not asked you for your input or given you enough facts for you to understand what he thinks is the issue.

If this is your starting point, the CEO may feel alienated, perceiving you as too academic or aggressive, and not as relatable or approachable. More likely, the CEO will choose a lawyer who communicates in a more straightforward manner, asks a lot of questions, and focuses on getting to know him, his company, and the particular challenges the company is facing.

Building business relationships is more about "relationships" than about "business." Finding areas of common interest, asking open-ended questions that reveal ways that you can be helpful to someone (beyond solving their legal problem), or learning more about their personal background is a much more effective way to build rapport and connection. Rapport and connection are essential in creating the trusted relationship that is the foundation of all business development. In later chapters, we will get into the specifics of that.

ANALYSIS PARALYSIS CAN UNDERMINE IMPLEMENTATION

Our ability to analyze problems and weigh risk are the hallmarks of being an effective lawyer. But when it comes to implementing a marking plan, we tend to overthink things.

In marketing, slow and steady wins the race. If you are second-guessing every LinkedIn post you write before you publish it or spending hours spinning your wheels about whether to follow up again with the banker you met at an industry function, you are not advancing your marketing plan.

If you keep procrastinating about sending out emails to past clients because you don't want to say the wrong thing, you are missing valuable opportunities to reconnect with the people who already know, like, and trust you. If you spend hours deciding whether to send nuts or a bottle of wine to thank a client, you may be missing the chance to make three more phone calls to potential referral sources. Similarly, overthinking what you put in a LinkedIn post will miss the point of LinkedIn. In social media, the most important thing to do is be consistent. While it is nice to be profound and cutting-edge sometimes, posting at least several times a month is even more important.

SKEPTICISM CAN ALSO BE A BARRIER TO RELATIONSHIP BUILDING

As a group, lawyers rank high on skepticism. That skepticism is crucial in the practice of law. Great lawyers think a lot about what might go wrong for their clients, so they don't take anything at face value. An effective lawyer anticipates risk.

But skepticism can be an impediment to building trusted relationships. And trusted relationships are the key to building referral relationships and in getting colleagues to adopt your vision. In late 2023, when many of us were starting to see the enormous potential of ChatGPT, I saw this in action. I was at a meeting with my networking group ProVisors. We spend a lot of time in ProVisors[2] trying to get to "know, like, and trust" each other so that we can make referrals.

I was in a breakout group with a number of lawyers and accountants, and we were supposed to be talking about a tool we are excited about in our businesses. I chose Fathom.video, an app that records, transcribes, and creates summaries, takeaways, and next steps. I explained how much time this tool saves me and how tools like Fathom are going to fundamentally alter how we practice law.

A lawyer in the group was the first to react. Instead of asking me questions about how I think Fathom will revolutionize the practice of law, he said to me "Oh, you have to watch out for wiretap statutes." His skepticism was front and center, and, needless to say, it didn't make me think more of him.

A client of mine who is the managing partner of a midsized firm was organizing a 20th-anniversary celebration for the opening of the firm. The event was held at a beautiful outdoor venue. The plan was to have partners invite their clients, but the firm also invited firm alumni (in-house counsel and partners who have lateralled to other firms), referral partners who serve their clients' other needs, and administrative staff.

It was clearly a great opportunity to showcase the firm and strengthen relationships. But some of my client's partners were not that happy about it. A few asked her why administrative staff needed to attend. Another partner asked why his clients would want to come. (He didn't want to waste their time.) Still other partners asked why they were inviting partners at other firms who are now competitors.

While the majority of her partners were excited about the event (it was in a great location), some did not see the party as a marketing opportunity. They only saw it as risky.

Fortunately, my client was able to be a good listener but talk her partners off the ledge. The event was a huge success.

A lawyer who wants to do a great job representing clients needs to wear her skeptic's hat when evaluating the other party's position in a deal or conflict. A lawyer who wants an accountant to refer corporate or real estate matters to him needs to build trust, not be skeptical of the accountant's choice of movies or restaurants.

---

[2] ProVisors is a national networking group comprised of trusted advisors who have at least ten years of experience in their discipline. The group includes many attorneys, accountants, financial planners, management consultants, and other professionals.

YES/BUT DISEASE

There is no question that a lot of lawyers like to argue. It is hard for many attorneys to take things at face value, and showing how smart we are is part of that. Challenging others is an occupational hazard that makes sense in the context of litigation or negotiating a deal. In other contexts, it can be downright annoying.

A partner who wants input from associates on how to create the best hybrid work policy should ask for feedback and say "thank you" rather than argue with the answer. Marshall Goldsmith, one of the grandfathers of executive coaching, suggests that saying "but" all the time ("I agree with you, but . . .") really shuts down conversation and is a deterrent to giving future feedback. Lawyers have a tendency to qualify a lot of their statements. While that may be good lawyering, it doesn't build social connection and encourage conversation.

If you want to build a practice, focus on relationships. If you want to build relationships, try validating more rather than challenging.

As lawyers, there is no shortage of topics that we like to debate. Which is the best pizza in town? Who is the best pitcher in the National League? Is Taylor Swift really that talented? (In my opinion, yes; but no more than a lot of other musicians who I like and follow.)

Feeling like you need to get in the last word is often not helpful in building trusted relationships.

YOU DON'T NEED TO PROVE YOU ARE THE SMARTEST PERSON IN THE ROOM

In law school, we are taught with the Socratic method. We are encouraged to be prepared, so we will look smart in class. We try to impress our professors by delivering eloquent analysis of case law. But in selling, *listening* is the key skill. You can't identify your client's pain if you don't listen.

People who are great listeners show they care. People want to hire people they know, like, and trust. You'll engender more trust and goodwill by being a great listener. That usually means listening 80 percent of the time and talking 20 percent of the time.

There will be plenty of time to give your opinion (and demonstrate your intellect) if the individual hires you. If you don't let your prospect talk, you may be rendering an opinion about the wrong problem. If you don't let your referral sources say what is on their mind, they will feel like you are not interested in them.

Listening in a nonjudgmental way is a great way to increase loyalty with your referral sources. "How can I be helpful to you?" We'll talk about that more in Part 2.

FEELING A SENSE OF URGENCY CAN ALSO BE AN IMPEDIMENT

Lawyers also rank high on the trait of urgency. Once again, a sense of urgency is a good quality for a lawyer who is trying to get a deal done (or meet any kind of filing deadline). But urgency may be a hindrance in social interactions.

If your college roommate is comptroller of a company that you want to do business with, it makes sense to get together for lunch. You can see if there is any opportunity to do work for him or some indirect way to be helpful. But if your friend tells you it's looking like a busy fall, don't reach out again a week later. Give it a few months so that you can get together when your friend is under less stress.

You may never end up doing work for the company. Or it may take months or years to cultivate the relationship. Or your roommate might end up at another company where he *can* give you work.

Another client of mine just landed his best client. He met her when they worked together in private practice. The lawyer had left their old firm ten years earlier and went to a company that already had intellectual property (IP) counsel. Periodically, my client invited his former colleague to meals, to panels where he was speaking, and he even invited her to be on panels. Ten years later, the client moved to another company, and she was finally able to send work to my client. That client is now his biggest client ever.

BE A RISK TAKER; BE MORE RESILIENT

As I already highlighted, being risk averse is an occupational hazard in the law. Lawyers as a group also rank low on resilience. We don't like to be criticized, and when we fail, we tend to blame it on ourselves.

A successful rainmaker takes a lot of chances and fails often. In baseball, a superstar is someone who bats.300 (failing seven times out of ten). You can be a superstar rainmaker if you bat.050 (landing business from five out of one hundred interactions you have).

This means that you will have a lot of "failure" along the way.

Really, what this means is that business development is a volume business. To be successful in generating legal work, you want to be meeting a lot of prospects over time. Some will never turn into clients; some will never even return your phone calls or respond to your emails.

The point is to not take any of this personally. (As a lawyer myself, I can say that this is easier said than done—but it is ultimately doable!) Practice telling yourself that these individuals may be busy and that their lack of response has nothing to do with you. Do that before you reach out. We will talk more about that in chapter 15.

Similarly, depending on which marketing activities you enjoy, you want to be publishing, speaking, posting on social media, or staying involved in professional or community activities over time. Many of these efforts will produce no direct results or results in the short run.

"I'M A PROFESSIONAL, NOT A SALESPERSON"

Professional identity can be an initial barrier to selling. In my own experience, I was raised by a father who was a math professor and a mother who was a school psychologist. I remember my father calling businesspeople "operators." Simply put, business was not respected in my household. Similarly, for many lawyers, selling feels dirty.

In my own 30-year journey, I've come to appreciate that selling legal services is nothing like selling used cars. If you like getting to know people, and if you like to find ways to be helpful, you can succeed in legal marketing. High-pressure sales don't work with high-ticket items such as legal services.

We assume people don't want to be sold. In reality, they do want solutions, and we can provide those solutions.

AUTONOMY AND CROSS-SELLING

As lawyers, we like our autonomy. We like to do things ourselves rather than delegate. We are less inclined to collaborate with other lawyers in our firm in marketing our practice, even where there are obvious synergies.

There is an element of risk aversion in this, as well. Will my partner steal my client? Part of this is structural. Many law firms are not good at institutionalizing clients or in sharing origination credit. You may not see much value in collaborating on marketing with your colleagues. You may prefer to control everything yourself.

If you are doing this, the odds are that you are leaving a lot of money on the table. Once a client is happy with your work and the service you provide, they will be more inclined to purchase more of your services. If you are part of a firm that has multiple practice areas, chances are good that other lawyers in your firm can do a much better job of servicing the client's other needs. But this can happen only when attorneys work collaboratively.

Our preference for autonomy can also be a barrier to seeking help. Sometimes, we are reluctant to seek out help because we see it as a sign of weakness.

But marketing, like the actual practice of law, is a skill in and of itself. Finding a mentor in your firm who can help you figure out where to best focus your own marketing energies can be invaluable in setting yourself up for future success. If you work at a firm that has a marketing department, learn to collaborate with them. And if you want to build your marketing skills more quickly, consider working with a coach. We talk about that more in chapter 25 at the end of this book.

START ACTING LIKE AN ENTREPRENEUR

In my experience, many lawyers are reluctant to spend money beyond things that are "necessary," like rent, utilities, IT, payroll, and office supplies. Marketing, however, requires an investment of time and money.

The dollars you spend today on conferences, web hosting, lunches, graphic design, or gifts may not bear fruit right away. In fact, much of your marketing budget will never yield any results. In the next chapter, we will dig deeper into that subject.

If you want to get marketing results, think in terms of investment, not in terms of expense. While most plaintiff personal-injury lawyers pay referral fees, lawyers in many other practice areas do not.

But paying referral fees on other types of work can act as a great lead-generation tool. I have a client who does corporate work for small businesses. He pays a 10 percent referral fee on all collections from that work. Many lawyers would see that as an expense. My client, who does think like an entrepreneur, sees it as an investment.

SUCCEEDING IN THE LAW REQUIRES MORE THAN BEING A GOOD LAWYER

Skepticism, risk aversion, urgency, a competitive spirit, and analytical thinking may make you a better lawyer. But turn off those tendencies when you are trying to build your network and strengthen your business relationships. While the quality of your lawyering will surely impact your career, being able to generate work, land the right job, or lead your firm requires different skill sets. And, in the long run, those things will have just as much impact on your career happiness as your technical abilities.

DON'T SHY AWAY FROM AUTHENTICITY

If you are fortunate enough to do what you love—something that reflects the authentic you—you will greatly increase your prospect for achieving your marketing goals.

If you are a litigator who doesn't enjoy a good fight or a corporate lawyer who has no interest in business, your chances of success in business development will drop.

If you hate the billable hour, maybe private practice isn't the best career choice for you.

Similarly, marketing as a lawyer doesn't mean you have to follow a prescribed set of activities that everyone else is doing.

In fact, engaging in activities that you genuinely enjoy and feel passionate about can be significantly more effective than forcing yourself to participate in ones you feel you "should" do.

I hear clients tell me all the time that they should [fill in the blank]. While "shoulds" are certainly a part of being a grown-up, when it comes to marketing, you are better off finding activities that you like—as long as these activities align with your objectives for building your reputation and building your network of potential clients and referral sources.

As I tell my clients all the time: "If you don't like golf, don't play golf."

This approach not only aligns better with your personal interests and strengths, but it also ensures that the energy you put into marketing your services is authentic and sustainable. Here's why embracing marketing activities that resonate with you personally and engaging in work that interests you is not just a preference, but a strategic choice for long-term success:

- ***Motivation***: You're more driven to consistently engage in marketing efforts that align with your interests.
- ***Authenticity***: Genuine enjoyment in what you do attracts potential clients and referral sources. Your passion will show, making you more relatable and trustworthy.

- ***Relationships***: Quality connections stem from shared interests or appreciation for your enthusiasm, not just from an exchange of business cards.
- ***Sustainability***: Marketing strategies that give you a sense of fulfillment are easier to maintain over time, ensuring long-term success.

In essence, choose both a niche and marketing strategies that mirror your passions and strengths. This approach not only enhances your well-being but also naturally attracts and retains clients. Let your unique qualities lead your marketing efforts, and you will see your practice grow.

Choosing to focus on a type of work because it is "hot" or pursuing marketing activities because that is what has worked for someone else is not a recipe for success. It may feel less risky, but in the long run, it is not a good strategy.

The only caveat is that sometimes it is worth trying things you "should" do; you may discover that they become things you *want* to do. As lawyers, we have a tendency to be skeptical about everything. Pushing past that skepticism can be worthwhile at times.

Push yourself to be social in a way that feels comfortable. As lawyers, we score low on sociability. But generating work does require you to connect with people. You can't build a practice by just sitting in your office and doing great work.

For most of us, large gala events are not an effective venue for building relationships. They are generally not a good substitute for one-on-one relationship building. Find the ways to socialize that fit your personality. Don't get caught up in the hype. A large event may give you a way to efficiently reconnect with people you already know. There is some value in that. But big gatherings are less likely to provide you with an opportunity to have meaningful conversations unless you are attending a multiday conference. In chapter 9, I talk about my return to live conferences and how that actually led to a great piece of work.

Now that you have the right mindset about marketing, let's focus on the practical ways that you can set aside your skepticism and get started.

CHAPTER 2

Ways to Market Yourself without Feeling Like a Salesperson

In my experience, studying law is a lot like learning how to play chess without being shown the chess board. That's actually how I felt when I started law school.

Like many 1L students, my understanding of the legal profession was shaped largely by pop culture. I had seen many courtroom dramas. At the same time, I had no real understanding of litigation. I had never heard of discovery. From day one, however, I was learning the Federal Rules of Civil Procedure. In essence, we were studying the rule book without being shown the playing field.

I believe that studying rules and case law before understanding the "game" is not a great way to learn. But associates do learn the practical ropes in the first few years in practice. For most attorneys, the first job is like an apprenticeship. That is not true, however, when it comes to marketing.

Once you have been a lawyer for a while, you begin to realize that to really advance in private practice, you need to learn how to market. Some law schools have started offering courses or seminars on topics like law firm management, entrepreneurship, and client development. But marketing is still not a standard part of the curriculum at most law schools. In addition, once in practice, many lawyers are given little guidance on how to develop a practice. In this chapter, we will discuss some of the basics to get you moving in the right direction.

If you are like me, selling is not part of your DNA. Going to law school was a way to become a professional rather than being a stepping stone to a career in business. You didn't learn a lot about marketing, and it's not something you are being taught in practice. It can feel daunting and uncomfortable to think about selling.

Marketing, however, doesn't have to be something you dread. It can actually be something that feels natural and comfortable. Perhaps it can be something you actually enjoy. That's what has happened to me in the years since I graduated from law school.

So where should you start and when should you begin? The short answer is that it is okay to start small and it is never too early to begin. Your first few years in practice are about learning the trade. If you are an associate at a firm, work will come your way. If you have your own practice, there may be more urgency to generate work right away. But even if you don't need to generate your own work right now, investing even a small amount of your time—while the stakes are low—will enable you to reap the rewards when it matters.

We'll go into much greater detail about that throughout this book, but for now, here are some preliminary steps to set yourself up for future success:

- ***Find the work that energizes you.*** You can't be everything to everyone, and trying to do so will only leave you lost in the crowd and drained. Start developing a niche that interests you. Choose something that makes you excited to get up in the morning. Whether it's family law, lending, employment law, trusts and estates, real estate, or intellectual property, carving out your own little corner in the legal world not only makes you stand out but also brings in the kind of work you'll enjoy. You may not be able to be selective when you are starting out. You may not be able to choose your assignments at first. But as you develop more experience, take note of what types of matters you like and what types of clients you enjoy representing. Focus on what gives you energy.
- ***Reconnect with old friends.*** Those late-night study sessions and hanging out in dorm rooms weren't just fun; they were networking gold. Keep up with your old buddies from school. You never know when someone's going to need a lawyer or recommend you to someone who does. Start reconnecting now when you don't need anything. Be curious about what your former classmates are up to.
- ***Be genuinely helpful.*** Networking isn't a transaction; it's about building a community. Offer your help freely without immediately looking for

something in return. While you can't give away your legal services for free, you can certainly educate people about the law more generally. Introduce a friend to a contact who can help that friend. Share your favorite movies, restaurants, vacation spots, or even just lend an ear. Refer them to another professional. What goes around comes around.

- ***Pick your fishing grounds wisely.*** If you're trying to catch lobster, you don't go to a lake. Choose activities and organizations that align with your interests and put you in the path of potential clients or referral partners. And if the thought of swinging a golf club doesn't excite you, skip the golf course. Find something that feels right for you and where you can be your authentic self.
- ***Embrace what you love.*** What is the best way to network? Do what you love. When you're engaging in activities that you're passionate about, your authenticity shines through, making you more approachable and relatable to potential clients and partners. That includes both the extracurricular activities you enjoy and the work you enjoy.
- ***Consistency is key.*** Carve out a little time each week for marketing efforts. Write an article, speak on a panel, go to a bar association meeting, or just catch up over coffee. Regularly putting yourself out there keeps the momentum going and makes the task less daunting.
- ***Social media savvy.*** Stay active online. A well-timed post or thoughtful comment can keep you on the radar of your network without feeling like you're shouting into the void.
- ***It's a marathon, not a sprint.*** Building a client base is a long game. Start planting those seeds now, without the pressure, and watch them grow into the practice you've dreamed of.
- ***Have fun with it!*** Marketing can be fun. Treat it like a puzzle to be solved or a game to be won. When you take the pressure off and start to enjoy the process, it stops feeling like work and starts feeling like part of the adventure.

Bar associations are often good places to start your marketing journey. Find a committee that interests you and attend the meetings. Get to know the players. Look for opportunities to write and eventually to speak. Even if writing or speaking is not your thing, meeting other lawyers who do the same types of work will make you a better attorney. Getting to know other lawyers in your practice area could open up marketing opportunities or even opportunities for referrals (e.g., when the lawyers you meet have conflicts of interest). Most importantly, bar associations will give you ample opportunity to start meeting other professionals and practice your networking skills. In Part 3, we will talk more about networking, why it is so important, and how to get more out of it.

Remember, the goal isn't to turn you into a sales machine overnight. It's about finding ways to market yourself that feel natural and enjoyable. By focusing on the types of problems you enjoy, staying connected, and being genuinely helpful, you'll not only build a successful practice but also have a great time doing it.

USE MULTICHANNEL MARKETING

In the last three years, I've noticed a trend. Simply put, my business is coming from everywhere. But I can't predict in advance which of my efforts will bear fruit.

In addition to hosting the *Counsel to Counsel* podcast, I write frequently, I participate actively in a terrific national business networking group called ProVisors, I give presentations, and I do a lot of free consultations.

I now attend ProVisors meetings all over the country since many are on Zoom, and I'm having many virtual one-on-one conversations with potential referral partners.

I frequently connect clients and professionals in my network with each other. I make referrals whenever possible, and I ask questions that may reveal needs that I can refer to other trusted advisors. In addition, I post regularly on LinkedIn and send out a monthly newsletter.

Periodically, I forward my own content directly to my clients or my referral sources. When I see an article or a cartoon that I think might interest someone, I forward that.

At the end of the year, I send nut baskets to some of my biggest clients and swag to others. Last year it was a Seckler Attorney Coaching matching pen and flashlight set. (Email me if you are interested!)

I do all these things because I enjoy them. Here's what I don't do:

- I don't play golf.
- I don't spend a lot of time at large networking functions (the exception I make is when I expect to see a lot of people I already know or if I'm going to a conference where there will be educational workshops).
- I rarely create videos of myself (although I'm starting to get more comfortable with that).
- I don't go to wine tastings.

- I'm not involved in any ongoing bar association committees in my state (although I am happy to plan a panel or a conference, and I do serve on the Board of the Career Center of the ABA).
- I'm not on any community boards.
- I never attend professional sporting events.

I make these choices because I know that what I tell my clients is true: If I try to get involved in things I don't enjoy and that are not authentically me, I'm not going to have fun.

More importantly, I'm going to make excuses about not participating; and if I do drag myself to a wine tasting or get involved in a committee where there is a lot more talk than action, my feelings are going to come out.

I've never played golf, but if I did, I'd probably be like Eeyore with a dark cloud over my head. I don't enjoy activities where I feel incompetent, and when it comes to exercise, I much prefer aerobic activities like squash or doing a Peloton class.

CULTIVATE RELATIONSHIPS THAT SUPPORT YOUR NICHE

As we already noted, in deciding what marketing and business development activities to use, the starting point has to be figuring out who is your ideal client and what is your niche.

Once you have figured that out, you want to use marketing tools that feel comfortable to you to build your reputation in that niche.

Ultimately, it is the relationships you build that will generate the work. So, the next step is to decide how to best reach the clients you want to represent or build relationships with other professionals who might come in contact with those clients.

Once you know that, choose the activities that give you the best opportunity to both build your reputation and your relationships with those individuals. But choose activities you like.

Put another way, if you want to marry someone Jewish, don't hang out at Catholic singles dances. And if you don't like dancing at all, join a book club, get involved in a nonprofit you care about, or find another activity that you do enjoy.

There is no one, right way to market. As long as you are involved in activities that you authentically enjoy and that help you build your reputation and deepen the *right* network, you can be successful.

Or as my father used to say: à chacun son goût (which is French for "to each his own").

IT IS HARD TO PREDICT WHERE YOUR REFERRALS WILL ACTUALLY COME FROM

Beyond that, you will have hits and misses, and frankly, you can't really predict where your work will come from as a lawyer unless you already have deep ties with institutional clients who have lots of ongoing legal needs.

Some of your activities will produce no results in the short run. Some will unexpectedly produce a lot of results.

Of course, at some point, you have to evaluate whether you are hanging out at the right dance. For example, if your target clients are Fortune 50 companies who are doing acquisitions of companies worth at least $500 million, then hanging out at the local chamber of commerce may not be a good venue for you.

I have a friend who does high-level general counsel searches for life sciences companies. A lot of her speaking has been at bar association meetings. More recently, she has realized that she wants to find ways to get more visible with HR executives and CEOs, the people who can hire her to conduct searches. She has shifted the focus to HR organizations and trade associations in biotech and medical devices.

Earlier in your career, it is fine to spend time speaking before legal audiences. As I've previously mentioned, bar associations are a good place to start building your reputation. Eventually, though, you want to go to the dance where you'll meet the right people. Unless lawyers are great referral sources for you, it may be time to change the channel or at least spend more time on another channel.

Even if an activity does seem to make sense, you should still reevaluate periodically how to best allocate your limited time.

In my case, I have work coming from many sources that I would never have predicted. One recent client who is in a career transition found me through a Google search (that probably has something to do with my podcast and the content I publish on my website).

One new client found me when his partner shared with him an article I wrote for an ABA publication. I don't even know his partner.

A general counsel I know who left Massachusetts more than ten years ago thought of me for leadership development for his number two. We are connected on LinkedIn, and he has seen a lot of my posts over the last few years. But we have not kept up directly.

Another new client is a lawyer I've known for a long time. We met when he was in a bigger firm. Recently, he began listening to my podcast, and after he attended a live streaming event that was sponsored by another attorney coach (I was one of four panelists), he finally reached out to me. He had just lost a big client, and he realized that it would be a good idea to ramp up his marketing activities; but he wasn't sure where to start.

Lately, ProVisors, a national business networking group, has been a great source of business. Someone in one of my affinity groups, and who I've been seeing for a couple of years, referred her partner to me for some career and marketing coaching.

An old client whom I had not kept up with joined ProVisors and reached out to me to start working together again.

Several years ago, I met with a lawyer who was trying to reenter the workforce after sailing around the world with his family. Back then, I was dividing my time between recruiting and coaching, but because of his situation, I couldn't place him. But he remembered me because I had given him some advice that ultimately helped him land a job. He really appreciated that. Recently, he referred a friend.

Finally, I picked up a good client from another attorney business development coach. The client had a scheduling conflict with the other coach. The other coach and I have a very good relationship, and he is someone I call when I have questions. He was introduced to me by someone else in my network who appreciates the value of *coopetition*, the idea that even our competitors can be good referral sources.

Of course, like every other professional, I've invested considerable time in activities that have produced no results. And that is to be expected.

Marketing is more art than science. And while lawyers often reflexively say they aren't good at it or don't like it, the truth is that there is something for everyone.

Lawyers are also risk averse and don't think like entrepreneurs. I've heard many attorneys question the value of giving presentations when a single presentation produces no leads.

WEATHER FORECASTING AND PREDICTING MARKETING SUCCESS

Snow day!

That is the text message I received one evening in December from my wife, who is the admissions director at a school.

By early evening, many of the school districts in Eastern Massachusetts had canceled school for the day because of predictions of a bad snowstorm that were supposed to hit overnight. Reports were that driving would be treacherous by morning.

That was the prediction. Looking out my kitchen window the next day, the reality was quite different!

Weather forecasting is as much art as it is science; but we all like to rely on it. We listen to the predictions and then make decisions based on those predictions. Sometimes those predictions are just wrong.

The same is true with marketing. We think that attending a particular industry conference will be a great way to build our network; but we find that there are limited opportunities to interact with the participants. The attendees are not really the people we want to meet.

We start sending out a monthly newsletter, but after a few months, we don't see any tangible results. Or we take a few clients or good referral sources to lunch, and suddenly the phone is ringing.

The point is that marketing, like the weather, is hard to predict. So if you want to really be effective in building your practice, understand that you may need to try ten things to have one of them work.

Go with the activities that you predict "might" work, and the things you choose should be authentic to you.

For most of us, using a multichannel marketing approach is the most effective way to ensure that we are covering our bases. We can't really predict what will yield results, and, in many ways, marketing is often the sum total of everything we do.

As lawyers, we like more certainty. With marketing, take some chances and understand that not everything will pan out. And that is okay. The important thing is to be slow and steady. Don't wait until your work slows down. The best rainmakers are always involved in some marketing activities. Over time, this will pay dividends. You just don't know which of your actions will produce the results you want—and deserve. Just make sure to reevaluate periodically and drop the activities that seem highly unlikely to produce results.

CHAPTER 3

22 Marketing Mistakes to Avoid

Fundamentally, growing a law practice is about relationship building. If you build your reputation in a well-defined niche and cultivate strong relationships with existing clients, prospective clients, and referral sources, your practice will grow over time.

While this may sound pretty straightforward, if you are like a "typical" attorney, there are a number of obstacles to overcome if you want to be successful.

Career identity is a large barrier. Most lawyers don't see selling as an honorable activity.

Beyond this, as lawyers, we are a risk-averse bunch. While selling and entrepreneurship are about "what are the opportunities," practicing law is about predicting "what might go wrong." In addition, according to Dr. Larry Richard, who has studied lawyer personalities extensively, lawyers generally score low on the personality trait of resilience. Because any kind of selling involves a lot of failure (you have to kiss a lot of frogs to find your prince), in order to succeed at legal marketing, you have to be able to move past rejection.

By observing many successful attorneys with large practices, I have come to appreciate that selling legal services is something that most attorneys can get better at. If you like getting to know people and if you have a service mentality, you can be successful.

In the 25-plus years I've been helping lawyers to achieve greater marketing success, I've noticed that there are some common mistakes that lawyers make in trying to grow their practice. Here is my list of 22 of those mistakes and what to do about them.

1. ***Saving marketing for a rainy day.*** In legal marketing, slow and steady wins the race. Because you can't predict when someone will need the services you are selling (or hear of someone who might have that need), it is important to be in front of your network on a regular basis, even when you are busy with client work. Doing *some* marketing all the time is much more effective than waiting until your workload slows down.
2. ***Analysis paralysis.*** It is impossible to know which marketing activities will bear fruit. Don't overanalyze whether any one activity will produce results.
3. ***Dividing your time into billable hours and non-billable time.*** Billable hours are the economic engine that drives most firms, but don't undervalue your investment hours (e.g., professional development, marketing, firm management, and self-care).
4. ***Doing something once and expecting immediate results.*** A single presentation before a professional association may generate work. But don't count on it.
5. ***Choosing activities that you don't enjoy.*** If you don't like golf, don't play golf.
6. ***Choosing a niche you don't like.*** If you are doing what you like, you will be more successful at it, and you will want more of it.
7. ***Only telling clients what can go wrong.*** One of the things lawyers quickly learn when they move in-house is that their internal clients want to know what they *can* do, not just what they *can't* do. Outside counsel should develop the same mentality. You are hired to manage risk. But you shouldn't be a deal killer.
8. ***Spending all of your time on marketing and none of it on relationship building.*** When lawyers are starting out, writing articles, posting on social media, and giving presentations may feel like a more comfortable way to market. But as your career progresses, it is the relationships you build that will lead to paying work. This is less true for plaintiffs' personal injury lawyers and attorneys who do other types of business-to-consumer (B2C) work. The clients who hire B2C lawyers represent a much broader cross section of the population. An individual who lacks a network of professionals may turn to Google, social media, or other search tools.
9. ***Failing to focus.*** You can't be remembered for everything. Choose a niche and focus on that (focus can be on type of client, industry, or type of legal work).

10. ***Talking about what you do rather than the types of problems you solve.*** Clients are looking for an attorney who has experience addressing their issues. For example, rather than saying *I do estate planning and administration*, say *I help middle-class families protect their wealth and pass on their estate while minimizing their tax burden. I generally work with clients who have between $500,000 and $5 million in assets.*
11. ***Doing it all yourself.*** Get help. You may think you know how to build a website, but is that a good use of your time when you are billing hundreds of dollars an hour? Sure, you can research the latest changes to the Google algorithm, but isn't it smarter to hire a digital marketing firm to advise you?
12. ***Forgetting to thank referral sources.*** It is so easy to send a quick email thanking your referral sources for thinking of you. It doesn't matter if the referral did not turn into a paying client. If there is a referral source who has been particularly helpful in sending you good matters, think about sending a small gift, especially at holiday time. If the matter was really not in your wheelhouse, thank them anyway and explain what types of cases would be a good fit.
13. ***Giving up too easily.*** How many times have you tried setting up coffee with good referral sources and gotten no response? Maybe they were busy when you sent the first email. Maybe it got caught in their spam filter. We'll talk a lot more about this in later chapters.
14. ***Talking too much.*** God gave you two ears and one mouth. People will be more impressed if you are a great listener. Listening is the only way to find out how you can be helpful to someone.
15. ***Hiding your successes.*** Clients want to hire lawyers who have experience and success in dealing with their issues. Tell stories that illustrate these successes.
16. ***Spreading yourself too thin.*** It is better to go deep with fewer activities than to have superficial involvement with a lot of organizations.
17. ***Failure to follow up.*** If you speak to a prospect, make sure to mark a date on your calendar when you will follow up with him or her.
18. ***Joining organizations but not really getting involved.*** It's nice to be able to say that you are a member of various trade associations, community groups, and nonprofit organizations. It's better to get to know individuals in these groups. As a partner once told my friend, "Don't be an empty suit." Sign up for a committee or volunteer to do something.

19. ***Thinking about tactics before strategy.*** As lawyers, we are really good at implementation. But before you decide on what marketing tactics will work best for you, it is important to know your ideal clients and what services you want to provide them. Of course you need a great website if you are launching your own firm; however, that should not be number one on your priority list. Think first about what kind of business you want to build. You may know how to put together a presentation or write an article on a hot topic. But that is the cart in front of the horse. Is the subject matter something you want to be known for? Are you speaking to the "right" audience?
20. ***Avoiding lawyers who do what you do.*** It's easy to look at lawyers who serve the same clients and think of them only as competitors. In truth, many lawyers get referrals due to conflicts of interest. If you build good relationships with the lawyers you meet on the other side of deals or in litigation matters, they are more likely to refer those conflicts to you. Similarly, if you choose your lane, you may find that a matter that is good for you is not good for someone you litigated against and vice versa. In addition, a healthy dose of "coopetition" is a way to market together (e.g., by appearing together on the same panels). Come to legal marketing with an attitude of abundance, not an attitude of scarcity; there is plenty of work for everyone.
21. ***Ignoring opportunities for cross-selling the firm's other services.*** It takes a lot of time and energy to build trust with clients. Once you have earned that trust, there may be an opportunity to serve other legal needs that they have. Are you fully aware of your firm's capabilities? Do you spend time talking to your partners about ways you can market together?
22. ***Failing to shift gears when something isn't producing results.*** While you want to stick with things for a while, at some point, it's time to cut bait. A client of mine was giving CLE presentations thinking that in-house counsel were attending. Eventually, he looked at the registration lists and saw that all of the attendees were lawyers in private practice who were essentially competitors. There is value in speaking to other lawyers who won't refer to you. It helps build your reputation to be the lawyer who is educating other attorneys. But moving on to other ponds is also important. My client is now focused on speaking with industry groups and non-attorney audiences.

I continue to make many of these mistakes. The goal here is not to strive for marketing perfection. Your success will change your behavior, but old habits are hard to change. In the next chapter, we will discuss why you want to put your marketing activities on autopilot.

CHAPTER 4

Mindlessness Is the Key to Marketing Success

"Action is the antidote to overthinking."

—*Unknown*

"80 percent of success is showing up."

—*Woody Allen*

While having a good strategy is an important starting point in your marketing journey, implementation is where the rubber meets the road. And this is where most lawyers (me included) get tripped up. That's where our analysis paralysis, skepticism, and fear of rejection really get in the way. Our tendency to overthink makes implementation a real challenge.

What is really called for, however, is a healthy dose of *mindlessness*.[1]

Figuring out who your ideal clients are and what are the ideal matters you want to work on is an important first step in building a marketing plan. Creating a niche practice area is an important way to ensure that you have differentiated yourself from the competition. Mapping out who are your key referral sources and how you can build relationships with these referral sources is essential. The process of coming up with a good marketing plan is anything but mindless. It requires deep thinking and actually plays to our strengths as lawyers.

[1] While I use the term "mindlessness" to make a point, I'm actually a big believer in the power of mindfulness. I meditate most mornings and belong to the Mindfulness in Law Society. If you are looking for a good path into mindfulness, check out one of the many smartphone apps that are available (I've used Ten Percent Happier, Calm, and Headspace). Even five minutes a day can help you reduce your stress and gain more focus.

But once you have a strategy and you move to implementation, it is time to shift gears. Successful execution requires consistency. Short bursts of activity followed by long breaks where you just focus on billable work is not a good way to keep your name top of mind with your network. Since it is hard to predict when your clients, prospective clients, and referral sources will hear about a legal problem that you might be able to solve, slow and steady wins the race.

LinkedIn[2] illustrates this point. LinkedIn is a great platform for sharing thought leadership and for staying top of mind. But the only way to stay top of mind on LinkedIn is to be there regularly.

The challenge for lawyers is to not let great be the enemy of the good. Posting on LinkedIn is not the same as writing a Supreme Court brief. Of course you want to sound intelligent and be accurate. Offering timely content is a nice way to demonstrate thought leadership. But finding ways to recycle evergreen content is more valuable than sheer originality and brilliance. Try mixing up your timely analysis with reposting things you've already written (as long as they still have value).

As it turns out, posting about the personal—and tying it to the professional—is one of the best ways to get engagement on LinkedIn (and on social media in general). My most successful posts have involved talking about wrecking my car, dog sitting (including a GIF with me and Buttons, a wonderful Australian Labradoodle), performing with a men's choir in a kilt, and COVID deaths in my family. I tied each of them to something business related, but clearly those got the attention of people who were scrolling.

In my experience, this is where lawyers get stuck the most. I've had clients perseverate over whether it made sense to post pictures from beautiful vacation spots.

FIGHTING THE LURE OF THE BILLABLE HOUR

One of the structural barriers to creating good marketing habits is the billable hour. As humans, we are wired for immediate gratification. In the case of practicing law, if there is work to bill, you will get the short-term reward of being paid (or making progress toward meeting your billable targets).

---

[2] Throughout this book, I make reference to LinkedIn because that is the platform I use most frequently, and it is a great platform for any lawyer who serves institutional clients or professionals. But Facebook, Instagram, and several other social media platforms can be particularly effective if you primarily represent individual clients.

Your marketing efforts, on the other hand, may not pay off for a long time, and as I noted, some of those efforts will not pay off at all.

In reality, though, ignoring marketing now can have significant adverse consequences in the future.

SHEER WILLPOWER IS INEFFECTIVE

Sheer willpower is unlikely to ensure that you will have the consistency you need to remain visible. Given the time pressures on most lawyers, the only way to build consistency is to create habits that don't require a lot of thought. In other words, marketing success requires a certain amount of "mindlessness" (e.g., every week, I'll call three of my referral sources, meet one for coffee, and post twice on LinkedIn; every quarter I'll give a presentation to an industry group; twice a month, I'll do a blog post, etc.). The specifics, of course, depend on your practice area, who you want to reach, and what you like to do. The bottom line is that you don't want to have to think about this all the time. Make your plan and then go on autopilot.[3]

There is a lot of research that demonstrates that it is forming habits and not sheer willpower that leads to change. If you're trying to lose weight, getting in the habit of not stocking high-calorie desserts in your freezer and pantry can help. Similarly, forming an exercise habit like going to the gym every Monday, Wednesday, and Friday morning is more likely to get you to the gym.[4]

Writing things in your calendar can also reinforce a habit and make it mindless. So does setting reminder flags in whatever contact manager you use so that you remember to circle back to leads, former clients, and potential referral partners.

It doesn't matter what system you use. The point is to have a system and then follow it. Your firm may actually have a good customer relationship management (CRM) system. If it works for you, learn how to use it. In my case, I use Outlook to keep myself organized. It's pretty basic but it works fine. I have reminders in my calendar to post on LinkedIn several times a week. When I send emails to networking contacts (e.g., after we have met for coffee), I bcc myself and then flag

---

[3] This is the premise of the book *Atomic Habits*. In his book, Cleary provides practical strategies for building good habits and breaking bad ones through small, incremental changes.

[4] For an interesting discussion on the importance of forming habits to implement change, listen to a great archive edition of *Hidden Brain* podcast, "Creatures of Habit." https://hiddenbrain.org/podcast/creatures-of-habit/

the email for follow-up in two to three months (or whatever is the appropriate length of time for that individual). One of my habits is that every month, I will release two podcasts and attend at least four meetings of ProVisors, my business networking group.

BUILDING A LAW PRACTICE IS FARMING, NOT HUNTING (IT IS A MARATHON, NOT A SPRINT)

Think of marketing as farming rather than hunting. But as I like to say, bring your shotgun just in case! You are building relationships and your reputation over time. A farmer can't just water her crops when she feels like it. Plants need water all the time. Similarly, having a habit of engaging in marketing activities regularly is the key to your success.

Part of reinforcing a habit can be having an accountability partner. That can be another lawyer you speak to in or out of your firm who is also trying to prioritize marketing. For some, having a coach provides the accountability.

Whatever you decide to do, create habits that get the ball rolling. You don't need to get to everything on your marketing to do list. Start with a few things that build your marketing muscles. You can always add to the list as you find comfortable ways to build your reputation and grow your network.

MEASURE YOUR ACTIVITY AND NOT YOUR RESULTS, BUT DON'T IGNORE YOUR RESULTS

Practicing mindlessness might suggest that you have no plan. That is actually not accurate. When I was trying to shed my "COVID-15" weight, my plan was to go to the gym at least five times a week, eat protein at almost every meal, decrease portion sizes, and reduce snacking. I paid the most attention to doing those things. But I did step on the scale several times a week as well to see if I was making progress toward my goal.

Are you getting referrals from certain people and not from others? The only way to know the answer is to track your referrals. At the same time, tracking the number of emails you send per week (without focusing on the results) is just as important.

AS LAWYERS, WE ARE GOOD AT FOLLOWING STEPS

As lawyers, we have a tendency to overthink. But we also excel at following routines and procedures. This is your marketing superpower.

Create lists of potential clients and referral sources. Make checklists of the marketing activities you will commit to. Put things in your calendar. Do this by yourself or with the help of a coach. Then stop thinking about your checklists and just execute. If you mindlessly engage in marketing activity on a regular basis, you will be successful.

Keep showing up and you will get the results you want.

In the next part, we delve into the most critical skill in legal marketing: listening.

PART 2

Can You Hear Me Now?

CHAPTER 5

Active Listening: Do I Really Need to Say This?

> "I've learned that people will forget what you said, people will forget what you did, but people will never forget how you made them feel."
>
> —*Maya Angelou*

> "People talking without speaking. People hearing without listening."
>
> —*Sound of Silence, Paul Simon*

Several years ago, the *New York Times* published an article by Deborah Tannen in which she described the term "cooperative overlapping." Tannen, a professor of linguistics at Georgetown, suggested that in New York, if you are not interrupting, you are not interested in the conversation.

After reading the article, it occurred to me that I'm in a mixed marriage. My wife is Jewish and from Ann Arbor, Michigan, and I'm Jewish and from New York.

Simply put, when I'm interested in a subject, I like to jump in and participate in the conversation. My wife, on the other hand, thinks that interrupting is rude. In the Midwest, it is more polite to let someone finish their thought before weighing in.

Since that time, I've been considering a bigger issue: Do I simply talk too much?

IN BUILDING BUSINESS RELATIONSHIPS, ACTIVE LISTENING IS KEY

I've been a student of active listening for more than 30 years. In 1990, I participated in my first mediation training and learned about the importance of giving parties a chance to feel heard. We practiced nonjudgmental listening and the art of asking open-ended questions. We learned that letting someone vent can go a long way in getting that person to start thinking about compromise.

Several years later, I learned that the same principles apply to coaching. A good coach asks a lot of open-ended questions and then listens with the intention of trying to understand. Good coaches do not focus on their own thoughts, feelings, reactions, and experiences when the client is speaking. A good coach asks questions to get coachees to articulate their goals and underlying beliefs and to identify roadblocks that are getting in the way of achieving those goals.

As I've come to appreciate, active listening skills are important not only in coaching and mediation. They are equally important if you want to build trusted relationships that will help you build your practice, advance your career, and be a more effective manager/leader.

Part of that means listening more and speaking less.

The deepest human need is to feel appreciated. When people believe that you are listening to them, they feel appreciated. This goes a long way to building the trusted relationships you need in order to generate work.

AS A GROUP, LAWYERS ARE NOT GREAT LISTENERS

In chapter 1, we discussed how the qualities that make lawyers effective in representing their clients (skepticism, aversion to risk, competitiveness, intellect, etc.) can get in the way when we are not actually practicing law.

In addition, one of the occupational hazards of being a professional is that people are paying us for our knowledge and wisdom.

This is particularly true in the practice of law where the ability to argue or state a position is often seen as the hallmark of good lawyering. Many of us like to talk because we think that is what will impress.

If you are representing a client in front of a tribunal, it is important to be persuasive and well spoken. But if you are trying to generate referrals from a good referral source, you need to remove your lawyering hat.

While some attorneys appreciate that representing clients and building a practice may require different communication skills, as a group, many of us are not good at shifting gears. We feel the need to explain ad nauseam in situations when no one really cares about the details. We fail to recognize that brevity might be a lot more effective in building trusted relationships. We fail to appreciate that *listening to understand* will get better results than *listening to respond*.

As lawyers, we like to show how smart we are. In reality, listening may be the best way to do that. There are times when we miss the mark by opening our mouths.

I was recently at a meeting for a committee I serve on. The chair suggested that we do an ice breaker. We were asked two questions. Who is someone you'd like to interview? Who would you like to play you in a movie? I immediately went into self-absorbed mode and started spinning my wheels to come up with responses while others were speaking. In the end, my answer was the same for both questions: Weird Al Yankovic (I like to write parody lyrics).

Unfortunately, I have utterly no recollection of what anyone else said. I wasn't listening. I was trying to get some laughs!

You may think you have a bad memory. But consider whether you are spending enough time listening to understand rather than listening to respond. If it is the latter, it could be impacting your memory for details about the people you meet.

So, how do we decide when to speak and when to keep quiet? One way is to apply the concept T.H.I.N.K. (The original source of the acronym is unknown, but it seems that it is used in some schools to teach children the skill of good listening.)

T.H.I.N.K. BEFORE YOU COMMUNICATE

Each letter in the acronym T.H.I.N.K. represents a question that you should ask yourself before you speak:

- ***T*** - Is it **t**rue?
- ***H*** - Is it **h**elpful?
- ***I*** - Is it **i**nspiring?
- ***N*** - Is it **n**ecessary?
- ***K*** - Is it **k**ind?

By considering these questions before speaking, individuals can avoid saying things that might be hurtful or unproductive and instead communicate in a more thoughtful and positive way.

Here are some other questions to think about in deciding whether something needs to be said:

- Are you being respectful?
- How might people interpret what you're saying?
- Is this appropriate for your audience? Maybe they don't share the same sense of humor or worldview.

I was on a panel a few years ago, and one of the speakers cited a book but gave the wrong name of the author. I thought briefly about correcting her. But it was a well-known book, I didn't think the audience would have any difficulty in tracking it down, and most importantly, I knew she would be offended. I didn't think it would be helpful, it wasn't kind, and it certainly wasn't necessary. I kept my mouth shut.

Humor can be a particularly challenging issue. If you are someone like me who takes pride in having a *good sense of humor*, it can be hard to hold back when a funny thought percolates into your consciousness. Getting someone to laugh is a great way to build your connection. But it can also backfire.

A few years ago, I was giving a presentation to a law firm about retirement, and I wanted to illustrate some stereotypical retirement activities that seniors might engage in. One of my slides showed a couple in their 70s gleefully playing a video game. I told the audience on Zoom that the couple was playing "Kill the Nazis." I'm pretty sure no one laughed. It happened to be a midwestern law firm and my New York sarcasm didn't translate well. Practice tip: Be very careful with humor on Zoom.

Not all topics are appropriate for all people. If I know that someone has children, especially adult children, as I do, I often use that as a way to connect. But if I know someone is single, I may avoid those topics unless he or she raises them.

Similarly, politics and religion can be dangerous topics to bring up, although, like humor, they can also be a great source of connection. We'll talk more on that in chapter 11.

STORYTELLING IS A GREAT WAY TO MAKE A POINT, BUT BE PREPARED

Storytelling is a great way to keep a listener engaged. But in most situations, if you have a good story to tell, keep it short. Think about what facts are necessary to make the point, and don't perseverate about non-material facts. This might take some preparation before you head out to a networking meeting.

Do you need to list the ten things that your client manufactures? Maybe in a court of law that matters. But maybe the accountant you are speaking to just needs to know that the two of you have synergies because you both serve manufacturing companies.

In a nutshell, many of us would often be better off saying a lot less (or sometimes nothing), particularly when we are not giving legal advice. Here are some common situations that we all find ourselves in and how you might want to navigate them:

- ***Being late to a meeting.*** If you are late to a meeting, just say you are sorry. In most situations, no one cares that you took your dog to the vet, that the vet was running late, and that after the appointment, you ran into an old friend who needed a lift.
- ***Listening to someone describe a bad experience.*** Being empathetic does not mean telling someone else about how you suffered the same injury, tragedy, or bad experience. I once worked for someone who, without fail, would share his own misfortune when someone shared theirs. When someone's dog has just died, they don't want to hear about how your dog died three years ago. There is something to the adage that "misery loves company," but be judicious in sharing your own misfortune when someone raises theirs.
- ***Responding to the question "what do you do" at a networking event.*** Recently, I was speaking with a lawyer whose specialty is data privacy. Pretty quickly, he got deep into the weeds and started talking about the regulatory agencies that govern the work he does. I was soon lost. He never stopped to check in with me to see if I was following him. If someone asks what you do, be succinct. Share only the skills that might be relevant to that individual. Talk about the people you help and problems you solve. If the person asks follow-up questions, by all means go into more detail. But don't give a ten-minute monologue.
- ***Receiving feedback.*** As a group, lawyers are terrible at receiving feedback. How often do we say "yes/but" when someone is letting us know what they think? We like to argue. We do not like criticism. But if we are truly committed to improvement (for ourselves and for our team), we want to encourage feedback and not shut it down. If someone gives you feedback, just say, "thank you." You can always get into a conversation about it later. Saying "thank you" does not mean you agree. The same is true when someone is giving us a compliment or giving us recognition. If someone compliments you, just say, "thank you." Don't minimize it or give commentary.

- ***Running a meeting.*** Being an active listener also means encouraging others to offer their opinion or ask questions. This is particularly true if you are running a meeting. Are there members of the client's team who have been silent and should be invited to give their input?
- ***When someone tells you something you already know.*** This is a particular pet peeve of mine. Is it really necessary to tell someone you already know a fact when they share it with you? Sometimes it is important. Often it is not. Saying you already knew something is more about proving how smart you are. In my observation, we do this a lot at lawyers.

  And last but not least:
- ***When advising clients or screening prospective clients.*** Giving advice is much more effective if we actually understand the problem before we jump in. While much of what I'm suggesting relates to communication beyond the actual practice of law, active listening is critical if you want to give good legal counsel. And in our effort to show clients or prospective clients that we are delivering value, many of us jump in too soon. Michael Bungay Stanier, a talented coach in Canada, calls this our "advice monster." As Michael suggests, the best way to respond when a client describes a problem is to say, "and what else?" and to keep doing this until we find out what the real problem is. Another way of thinking about this is the expression "prescription without diagnosis is malpractice." When clients are describing their problems, we should listen more to better understand their issues. Otherwise, we may be solving the wrong problem (or missing the bigger problem).

God gave us two ears and one mouth for a reason. If you spend more time exercising your ears, your law practice will grow, your career will advance, and you will be a much happier manager. And you'll be a better lawyer as well!

CURIOSITY KEEPS THE CLIENTS

A few months ago, Barry Horwitz, a friend of mine who does strategy consulting, posted on LinkedIn about the importance of asking good questions. His basic premise is that if we want to do a good job (as consultants, lawyers, etc.), digging deeper and challenging assumptions is critical.

He also pointed out that as adults, we ask far fewer questions than we did when we were young children. In part, that's because we want to appear smart. (According to Barry, a 4-year-old will ask 400 questions in a day while a

44-year-old will ask only 6. As the grandfather to a preschooler, he is actually an authority on the subject.)

Asking good questions is good for our clients. If we fail to probe deeply enough, we may end up solving the "wrong" problem. Doctors like to talk about the "presenting problem." Good medicine requires doctors to figure out the "underlying problem."

As it turns out, asking great questions is also great marketing.

One of the best ways to grow your practice is to deepen your relationships with existing clients. Doing a competent job as a lawyer is a given. That may very well keep the client coming back for more. It may result in good referrals.

But if you want to cross-sell other services to clients, you need to ask a lot of open-ended questions. And listen to the answers!

What other challenges are they seeing in their business? What else are they working on now? Do they need referrals to any other professionals (e.g., an accountant, a graphic designer, a real estate broker, or a financial planner)?

Asking good questions is the way we uncover other needs that clients may have. Some of these may be needs that other lawyers in our firm can handle. Some of these may be needs that our referral partners can handle (which, of course, strengthens our relationship with these referral partners).

Some of these needs may simply be personal (travel tips about a country you have visited, a good movie recommendation, a good plumber, a willingness to speak to their son who is applying to your alma mater, etc.).

Even if you are not selling your own services or the services of your firm, when you share resources with clients, you are deepening your relationship. The same is true when you are out networking with accountants, realtors, bankers, and other professionals who you want to cultivate.

Asking good questions is really the key to selling legal services. The good news is that the other person is doing most of the talking. It is like doing direct examination. The client has the answers. The client knows what they need. You are just trying to get them to articulate it.

And if they happen to have a need where you can be helpful, then (and only then) you can tell them that you'd be happy to help.

DO I HAVE YOUR UNDIVIDED ATTENTION?

A few years ago, I called a former colleague to get some advice. I really valued his opinion, and he is someone I knew I could count on to be frank. Unfortunately, he is also someone who likes to multitask (and someone who is easily distracted).

In fact, almost every telephone conversation that I ever had with him ended the same way: "Oh, I'm sorry Steve. I really need to take this call."

On that occasion, I decided to nip the problem in the bud. I needed an uninterrupted block of time to get his feedback on something so I asked him when I could have his undivided attention for 20 minutes. He quickly wrote back and said that he would be driving to New York and that I could reach him the next night after 7 p.m.

I wrote back to him and pointed out that talking in the car means that he would be dividing his attention between me and all of the other cars on the road. Nonetheless, I decided to take what I could get.

The following night, I called him at the appointed hour, and he answered right away. As we began our conversation, I was able to put aside my own bias (i.e., that talking on the phone while driving means that you are not fully engaged in either driving or talking). But a few minutes into our phone call, it became apparent that we were not alone. He was driving to New York, yes; but he had his whole family in the car. When his daughter needed to throw up, that was the end of the call.

Giving someone your undivided attention is not easy in our wired world. We are surrounded by many sources of distraction throughout the course of our workday, and email, text messages, and internal communication channels like Slack have changed our expectations about how quickly we must respond. Before the internet, the phone was a potential interruption at meetings that took place in the office. Now smartphones, laptops, and other digital media constantly vie for our attention wherever we are.

The upside is that we don't have to finish our conversation before we set off for our next destination. But we are fooling ourselves if we think that the person on the other end of the line is getting our full attention when we check our email, scroll through social media, or get in a car to drive somewhere while we are still talking to them.

This may not always matter. Sometimes, a conversation is simply a chance to quickly pass along some information. And as a self-employed individual, I greatly value the flexibility that comes with being able to leave my office without having to risk missing an important phone call or email message.

But this has to be done with balance. We harm our relationships when we refuse to give them our full attention. In contrast, we really strengthen our relationships when we listen with no interruption. And it is by being a great listener that we build our referral networks.

So what is a busy professional to do? For starters, try turning your smartphone to silent when you meet with your clients and referral sources face-to-face. Setting the phone to vibrate will be less of an intrusion if you happen to receive a message during the meeting, but in all likelihood, a little buzz in your pocket is still likely to distract you.

If you are speaking on the phone and don't need your computer, then don't face your computer, or at least close all of the windows that are likely to distract you. Turn off any audible alerts that tell you when an email message arrives.

There is great power in giving other professionals your undivided attention. Good relationships are not based on efficiency—they are based on trust, something that can be built only when you make the necessary investment of time.

Try giving one of your professional contacts your undivided attention and see what happens. Ask open-ended questions and listen. Let the other person do 80 percent of the talking. You'll be amazed at what you learn. In addition, they'll know that at least for the time you are speaking to them, you think they are worthy of your undivided attention.

AIM FOR LEVEL 2 OR LEVEL 3 LISTENING

In the book *Co-Active Coaching*, the authors talk about three levels of listening.

Level 1: Internal Listening

This level is focused on the self. When you are listening at Level 1, you are mainly aware of your own thoughts, opinions, judgments, and reactions. The focus is on how the conversation relates to you. For example, while someone is talking, you might be thinking about how their words affect you or how you will respond. This type of listening is typical in everyday conversations where we prioritize our own feelings and reactions over the other person's message.

Level 2: Focused Listening

At Level 2, the focus shifts entirely to the other person. You are deeply attuned to what they are saying and how they are saying it, picking up on their words, tone, emotions, and body language. There is a strong sense of empathy, and you are paying close attention to their experience. Level 2 listening is fully present and involves trying to understand the speaker's message and perspective. With level 2 listening, you are asking a lot of open-ended questions in order to deepen your understanding.

Level 3: Global Listening

Level 3 is the deepest level of listening. It encompasses not only what is being said but also the surrounding context, such as energy, mood, and environment. Here, you listen with your intuition, noticing subtle cues, unspoken emotions, and the overall atmosphere of the conversation. It involves being aware of the energy in the room, the shifts in the speaker's tone, or other nonverbal signals.

If you want someone to feel like you are really listening to them, try to engage in level 2 or level 3 listening. Not only will you gain a better understanding of who they are, what they need, and how you can help them, but you will build trust and rapport that will increase the likelihood that they will retain you, refer work to you, or remember you when an appropriate opportunity arises.

A NOTE ABOUT ADHD

There is a growing awareness that the rate of attention-deficit/hyperactivity disorder (ADHD) is much higher in the legal profession in comparison with the general population. One law firm, Goodwin Procter, has actually set up a program to support lawyers with this diagnosis.

This tendency makes alerts from cell phones, social media, Slack channels, email, and text messages a particular challenge. For someone with ADHD, it is extra difficult to give your undivided attention to another individual.

If you are someone with ADHD (or you believe you might be living with ADHD), you should seek out professional help. You may need to work a little harder to remove the distractions from your life. Taking mental breaks is probably more important for you. There are also other strategies that you can employ to stay focused.

A good starting place if you want more resources is to check out one of the lawyer assistance programs in your state. In Massachusetts, there is Lawyers Concerned for Lawyers, which offers free and confidential consultations to attorneys experiencing mental health challenges. For additional information, refer to the American Bar Association Commission on Lawyer Assistance Programs, which provides an overview and links to various state programs.

The good news is that people with ADHD tend to be more creative. You can use that creativity to generate more ideas for reinforcing social connection. You can also use your creativity to generate more ideas for building your reputation and increasing your visibility.

In addition, people with ADHD have the ability to hyperfocus at times. This can offset your tendency to be drawn away from conversations.

We all need to work hard at minimizing distractions. We live in a world where there have never been more ways to lose our focus. Whether you do have ADHD or are simply a heavy user of technology, taking the time to figure out how to stay more focused will help you build stronger social connection. That in turn will have a very positive effect on your ability to cultivate your relationships with clients, potential clients, and referral sources.

CHAPTER 6

How NOT to Communicate Like a Lawyer

> "When it comes to attorneys, every statement is a potential argument waiting to happen."
>
> —*Unknown*

Some of our greatest strengths as practicing lawyers can turn into liabilities when we turn to marketing. Our attention to detail, our skill in crafting persuasive arguments, and our ability to identify risks are all assets in the practice of law. They can hinder us in building solid referral networks.

Success as a lawyer requires attention to detail. If you file a discovery request and fail to include a category of business records, you may not get the documents you need to win your case.

If you draft a contract that is missing definitions of key terms, then your client may have an ambiguous deal.

No matter what your area of practice may be, part of your job as a lawyer means getting the details right.

While effective lawyering requires meticulous attention to detail, success in marketing your legal services requires another set of skills. Marketing success depends on being able to effectively communicate the big picture. In marketing, too much detail can dilute your message.

Listening, as we have already discussed, is also key. If you fail to take the time to be a good listener, you will miss great opportunities to be helpful and to strengthen your relationships. You may be trying to solve the wrong problem.

FREQUENTLY, CLIENTS AND POTENTIAL REFERRAL SOURCES JUST WANT TO KNOW WHAT IS AND WHAT IS NOT POSSIBLE

An employment attorney I work with was invited in to present to a potential client about handling their HR compliance. My client's firm has proprietary software that helps to streamline certain aspects of HR compliance, and my client was excited that they were invited in after responding to a request for proposals (RFP).

I debriefed with my client afterwards and as it turns out, she and another member of her team spoke for nearly one and one-half hours with little break.

I asked her whether she had begun the presentation by asking the potential client questions about what they were looking for. Unfortunately, she did not, and unfortunately, the company went with a different law firm.

My client agreed that she probably gave them too much detail about her firm's software. She was excited about the tool her firm had created, and she wanted to convey that excitement to the chief human resources officer and general counsel.

A better approach (which she will use in future pitches) is to focus more on finding out what is important to the client, what is missing from their compliance process, and what aspects of her firm's technology is of greatest interest.

Limiting details does not come easily to many lawyers. As a junior associate, you learn to be thorough and are criticized for not paying enough attention to detail. Partners expect that the work you submit should be precise and as close to perfect as possible. Most partners highly value associates who they consider detail oriented.

Your non-attorney clients, on the other hand, are probably less concerned with the details or the legal analysis that are the stock of your trade. They want to know that you can get the details right; but they don't necessarily want to hear a lengthy explanation about how you arrived at your conclusions.

Similarly, when you are at professional gatherings and have the chance to meet potential clients, you are much better off introducing yourself in a succinct fashion. Businesspeople are more likely to connect with you and remember you if you aim for brevity when you describe what you do.

A well-crafted sentence or two about how you provide value to your clients is much more likely to open up a conversation than a lengthy discourse about the deals you have been working on.

More about that later.

WE CAN RETRIEVE INFORMATION MORE EFFECTIVELY IF WE HAVE A PLACE TO "FILE" IT

Think of the brain as a giant filing cabinet. If information has no particular place to be filed, it becomes difficult to retrieve. The same is true if there is too much information to file.

By choosing a focus and keeping it brief, we make it easier for our contacts to help us by giving them a place to file the information that we provide. Once information is properly filed, it is more likely to be remembered.

It comes down to the adage that "less is more." Think about how advertisers boil their message down to something simple like "Just Do It, Nike." If you wanted to sell sneakers, you would not create a ten-minute commercial explaining in detail your manufacturing processes and how you procure inexpensive rubber to keep your prices low (although this is something that you might document in a prospectus or in other securities filings).

FOCUS DOES NOT PRECLUDE YOU FROM OFFERING A VARIETY OF SERVICES TO A VARIETY OF CLIENTS

I had lunch the other day with a partner of a small law firm. I have always considered this individual to be a bankruptcy lawyer; but as we got caught up, he described himself as someone who does real estate and corporate finance. I then discovered that back in the 1990s, he used to describe himself a commercial litigator.

Was he lacking in focus? Was his marketing message weak?

Many of the clients that I coach have difficulty in choosing a marketing focus. The common fear that I encounter is the fear of missing opportunities; the mistaken belief is that if you don't say everything you do, you may miss the chance to serve someone who has a problem that you can solve. In reality, when it comes to marketing, less is more.

While it is true that less is more, this does not mean that your marketing message must remain fixed over time. As the economy shifts and as the law evolves, lawyers need to be able to shift as well. What may be a hot specialty today may no longer be needed tomorrow. This will be true throughout your career.

Coupled with the need to be nimble over time is the need to recognize that finding the right way to describe your services may involve some trial and error.

In other words, in order to maximize your marketing effectiveness, you may need to test-market a few phrases before you settle on one that works.

Political strategists and marketing consultants understand this. The words you choose to describe what you do can have a great impact on how you are perceived and whether you will be remembered. (Why do you think that Republicans now refer to the estate tax as the "death tax"?)

The goal, of course, is to deliver a focused message about what you do (i.e., one that makes you memorable and differentiates you from other lawyers). When you find a message that works, stick with it. Repetition is essential in marketing. But be aware of the need to evolve as the law and the marketplace for legal services evolves. Otherwise, you may find yourself trying to sell buggy whips to consumers who want hybrid cars.

The following diagram illustrates this point. Figure out who your ideal client is and what services you provide to those clients. That's where you should focus your messaging. Understand what other work you do that you are not going to market. And know what work you don't do and will refer to other lawyers inside or outside of your firm.

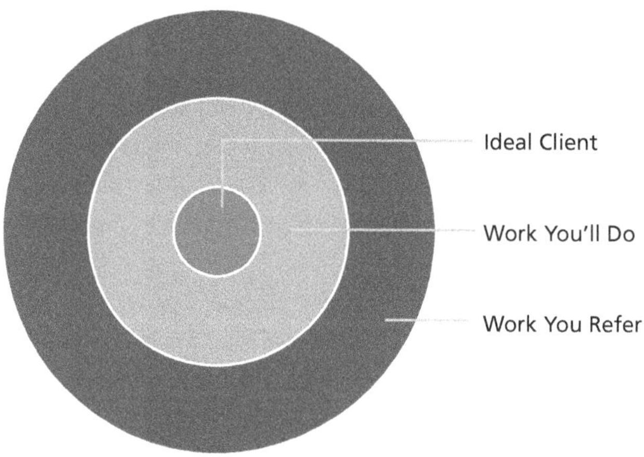

TALK TO POTENTIAL CLIENTS IN A LANGUAGE THEY CAN UNDERSTAND

Unless you are speaking to another lawyer who happens to share your subject matter expertise, keep shop talk to a minimum. Most clients have no real way to judge your technical proficiency, and most non-attorneys will not be interested in the subtle nuances of your work. They will measure your value by the way you communicate.

If you communicate in a clear and responsive way and show that you really understand their business, they will be impressed. If you talk about the US Internal Revenue Code, you will probably lose them.

BY SIMPLIFYING YOUR MESSAGE, YOU ARE OPENING THE DOOR TO FURTHER DISCUSSION

It is important to maintain your integrity in all your communications with existing or prospective clients. But that does not mean you have to be entirely transparent when you talk about what you do.

If you are a litigator, talk about how you successfully defended a company in a trade secrets case. Don't talk about how the case was originally filed in state court in Virginia and removed to federal District Court in Massachusetts, at which point you were retained as local counsel and then filed a motion for summary judgment and asked for punitive damages.

As long as leaving out details does not distort your competencies, you should feel comfortable with sticking to the highlights of how you helped your clients. If the other individual is interested in getting more details about how you solved a legal problem, you can always add this information in later.

Similarly, when you tell stories, they don't have to be brand-new stories. If someone asks "what's new," you can still talk about the great victory you had six months ago. The statute of limitations on good news is a lot longer than you might think.

In the right context, jargon is sometimes appropriate. When you are talking to another lawyer who practices in the same area, it makes sense to talk shop. On the other hand, be mindful of your audience.

I attend a lot of networking meetings through my business networking group ProVisors. I listen to a lot of lawyers introducing themselves and what they do. There are some who have figured out a succinct way to describe the clients they serve and the problems they solve. Many feel compelled to give a laundry list of their areas of expertise. Some get caught up in wanting to accurately describe their competency in working on a particular type of matter. When this happens, I find myself tuning out a little, and I suspect that other lawyers and professionals who are at these meetings have the same reaction.

CHOOSE YOUR BATTLES

One of the classic stereotypes about lawyers is that we like to argue about everything and prove that we are right. Again, that is a skill that often serves our clients well (although not always). But in networking situations or in conversations with friends and family, it can be downright annoying!

If we are skeptical about everything, we destroy trust. Dr. Larry Richard explains that skepticism is a reciprocal trait. If I am skeptical with you, you are going to be skeptical with me. In short, if you are trying to build a relationship with a potential referral source, don't argue about which restaurant has better onion rings.

The same is true even when talking about substantive legal issues. If the purpose of the conversation is just to get to know the other person, pay more attention to getting to know the other person. Resist the temptation to dispute something the other person is saying. Even if you are "right," you may be destroying the trust you are trying to build.

DON'T BE A DEBBIE DOWNER

According to Martin Seligman, the father of positive psychology, lawyers are natural pessimists. This comfort with catastrophizing can frequently carry into our personal lives, with negative ramifications. The results include lawyers experiencing high rates of depression, burnout, alcoholism, and divorce.

Needless to say, this is also not good for building business relationships.

While there are many coaches in my network who believe that lawyers can change their mindset and think more optimistically, I'm actually somewhat skeptical about our ability to alter our default thinking (very meta!).

But I do believe we can get past our default reactions and act in a more constructive way, and that is a lot of what I'm trying to convey in this book.

As a former New Yorker who often suffers from Eeyore syndrome, I've had to train myself to pause before I react. Therapy, coaching, and mindfulness meditation have all been very helpful in this regard. Getting the positive results I want has also reinforced my behavior.

To give you an idea of what I'm talking about, in the summer of 2022, I received a phone call at noon asking if I could speak in person that evening to a group of lawyers in Boston. A speaker had cancelled at the last minute.

My inner dialogue then went something like this: "Sigh. I need to get dressed. I need to take a shower. I need to drive into Boston. Where am I going to park? Do I even want to speak to this group?"

But I paused and thought about it for a moment. I hadn't done a live presentation since the start of the pandemic. I had a number of canned presentations that I could use. While this wasn't exactly my target market, it would be a good opportunity to start doing live presentations again.

So I said yes, put together my presentation, hopped in the shower, parked for $9 in Boston's Financial District after hours, and had a great time.

As lawyers, we have some great strengths. We should leverage those strengths to advise and protect our clients. But when it comes to building the relationships, we need to grow our practice, and we need to rethink our communication style. While changing your mindset is great, it is not essential. What is essential is that you change your behavior.

Put another way, don't be like a Dementor (the character in Harry Potter who sucks all of the joy out to the room).

CHAPTER 7

Turning Business Contacts into Business

In later chapters, we'll continue to explore ways to build your business network, but at this point, you may be wondering: how do I generate work from all of these relationships I'm building? The starting point is being a great listener. The next step is to get your prospects to articulate their needs.

MANY LAWYERS HAVE THE WRONG INSTINCTS ABOUT SELLING

You may think that it is your job to convince a client to hire you. While this is often more effective than simply being passive (i.e., deploying the strategy that "If I do great work, I'll get more work!"), it is even more effective to *open up the conversation* when we are speaking with a potential client than it is to try and *close* the business.

I talk to my clients about four modes of communication: passive, aggressive, assertive, and passive aggressive. The first three are most relevant when it comes to business development. (Passive-aggressive communication is an issue that I address more in leadership coaching.)

"Passive communication" is hoping the client will see the value in hiring you just because you have done good work in the past (i.e., you describe your experience without really starting a conversation or asking a lot of questions). You wait for the client to ask for your help.

"Aggressive communication" is telling the prospect that you have the solution and that they need to hire you, or bad things will happen—before taking the time to truly understand their problem and finding out what they really want. While zealous advocacy may be good for your client when you are representing them in a matter, it's often not effective in getting a client to hire you for a matter.

In true Goldilocks fashion, you want to take the middle approach and use "assertive communication" in order to get the best results when speaking to prospects. Assertive means expressing your point of view in a way that is clear and direct, while still respecting the opinion of the other person. Conducting a "friendly deposition" is the way you will learn what you need to know in order to address the concerns of the other individual or business.

ACTIVE LISTENING IS AN ESSENTIAL SKILL IN YOUR TOOLBOX

The starting point in assertive communication is active listening. Until a prospect can articulate that they actually need help, and until you fully understand the problem, it is premature to start telling them how you charge for your services. Until you truly understand the issue, it is too soon to suggest that you have the solution.

Much of this is well described in the classic book *SPIN Selling*, which was first published in the late 1980s. *SPIN Selling*, which was based on in-depth research involving thousands of sales transaction, provides a useful framework for thinking about selling your services as a lawyer.

With SPIN, the starting point is to ask a lot of questions and listen to the answers. Get a handle on the *situation* (S). Next, identify the *problems* (P) that the individual or business faces. Have them articulate what are the *implications* (I) if they do not address these problems. Finally, ask them what it would mean to them if they could solve the problem, or in terms of SPIN, what would be the *need-payoff* (N).

Sometimes a client will come to you with a very clearly defined need (e.g., they are buying a house, and they need a lawyer to help with the closing; they just became a parent and would like you to draft a will and related estate planning documents to protect their family; they are starting a new job and need a lawyer to review an employment agreement). If that is the case, you may not need to do a lot of digging to uncover the real need (but make sure to do at least *some* digging, even when the matter seems straightforward!).

More often, the need is not apparent at the outset. When this happens, asking a lot of open-ended questions can give you a much better handle on what the problem is. Paraphrasing and confirming you correctly heard what they said will build trust. Asking good follow-up questions that feed off of their answers does the same. Maintaining good eye contact and open body language is also important.

For example, someone may come to you saying they would like to sue their landlord. The roof is leaking and there is a problem with pests. But a deeper inquiry might reveal that they just want to get out of their lease. They actually have no appetite for a lengthy battle. They simply want to live in a safe place and would like a lawyer to advise them of their rights and potentially write a letter to their landlord.

A business owner comes to you and asks you to draft a partnership agreement. But a deeper dive reveals that keeping it an independent contractor relationship makes more sense. He actually has a bad track record when it comes to working with business partners and he needs someone to create a contract that spells out their business relationship without inadvertently violating any employment laws. He may also need help with his own client contracts.

It is important to establish what the real issue is before suggesting that you are the right lawyer to represent them. You may be trying to solve the wrong problem or solve it in a way that is not of interest to the prospect. If you delve deeply enough, it may be a matter that you would be better off referring to another attorney or even another professional.

By demonstrating that you are a great listener and by getting the individual to clearly articulate the problem, you have a much better chance of getting that individual to hire you.

Rather than showing how smart you are, use your abstract reasoning to get the prospect to state the problem and solution.

A crucial part of SPIN Selling involves guiding the prospective client to articulate their problems and the value of potential solutions themselves. This approach leverages the client's own words and insights to build a stronger commitment to purchasing the lawyer's services. By doing so, it effectively uses the principles of the endowment effect to the seller's advantage (the idea that we place more value in ideas that come from us). Here's how it works:

1. **Problem Questions:** By asking well-crafted problem questions, the lawyer helps the client to identify and verbalize the specific issues they are facing. When the buyer states these problems themselves, they are more likely to

acknowledge their significance and feel a sense of ownership over the identification of these issues. Think about it in terms of "direct examination." Ask a lot of open-ended questions that get the client talking.

2. **Implication Questions:** These questions help the client to explore the broader impact and consequences of their problems. When the client articulates the implications, they gain a deeper understanding of the urgency and necessity of addressing these issues. This process also enhances their emotional investment in finding a solution.
3. **Need-Payoff Questions:** These questions prompt the client to describe the benefits and value of resolving their problems. When the client identifies and states the advantages of the proposed solution, they begin to internalize the benefits, making them more likely to commit to purchasing the lawyer's services. This stage is critical as it shifts the focus from the problem to the positive outcomes, aligning with the client's goals and motivations.

By guiding the buyer through these stages, SPIN Selling taps into the endowment effect by having the buyer "own" the discovery of their problems and the value of the solution. This ownership makes the client more committed to the decision to retain you, as they feel that they have actively participated in the problem-solving process and arrived at the conclusion themselves. This approach not only builds buy-in but also fosters a sense of trust and partnership between the lawyer and the client.

In summary, get the client to clearly articulate the need and ask enough questions so that you are confident that this is something you are competent to handle. Most importantly, LISTEN!

"IT DEPENDS" IS A BAD STARTING POINT

Once you have gotten clarity about what the prospective client wants help with and that they are committed to solving the problem or addressing the issue, now it is time to ask them: "What questions do you have for me?" They'll probably say one of several things: "Is this something you can help me with?" " Do you think I have a case?" "Can you tell me about your services?" or "How do you charge for your services?"

If they ask any of those questions, you know you are making progress in getting this individual to hire you.

While it is too soon to weigh in with your legal opinion (they haven't formally retained you yet), you do want them to walk away from the conversation feeling like you will be able to take care of them. That doesn't mean that you have all the answers or that you can assure them of the result they want; but you can explain to them that you have a lot of experience with matters like theirs and you can promise them that you will do your best to get them what they want or need.

If you respond with the quintessential lawyer answer "it depends" (e.g., when they ask if you can help them), that is unlikely to instill confidence in your abilities.

Imagine that you are feeling a sharp pain in the back of your head. You go to the emergency room, and you ask the doctor if she can help you. If she says *I'm not sure, I've never seen a case like yours*, that is unlikely to inspire confidence. But if she looks you in the eye and assures you that she will do her best to get to the bottom of it, then you are going to have much more confidence in her competence.

Clients want to know that you will take care of them and that you will be responsive. Generally speaking, people who hire lawyers do not really know whether you are a good lawyer. But they do know how you make them feel.

If you are like most lawyers, the reason you say *it depends* is that you don't want to be wrong. Your analytical brain is thinking "there are a lot of ways that this might turn out and I don't want to promise something that isn't certain."

But the prospective client is just looking for someone they can count on to represent their interests and advise them competently.

Try responding with something like: *We've handled many cases like this before. I can assure you we will do everything in our power to make sure that your legal rights are protected.*

IF THE MATTER SEEMS COMPLEX, SCHEDULE A FOLLOW-UP MEETING

If the matter at hand is straightforward like a real estate closing, it is fine to quote a price at that first meeting. But if there is any ambiguity about how much work will be involved, you are much better off scheduling a follow-up meeting to present the client with a proposal.

Setting a follow-up meeting serves several purposes. First, it gives you a chance to really think through what might be involved. It shows the client that this is not necessarily as straightforward as they might believe.

Setting a follow-up meeting also demonstrates how serious the prospective client is about hiring you. If they say *let me get back to you on that*, this is a good sign that you may never hear from them again and that it is not worth your time to follow up with them.

If they agree to a follow-up meeting, they are demonstrating some commitment to working with you (and showing that they will be a good client to work with).

The key is to make sure the prospective client understands the value of hiring you. A follow-up meeting is a chance to demonstrate to them what they will get if they hire you.

LOOK THEM IN THE EYE AND TELL THEM YOU CAN HELP THEM WITH THEIR ISSUE

While I've already cautioned that it is important to remove your advocacy hat when you are first meeting with a prospect, when it is clear that they have a problem, that they want the problem solved, and that you are the right person to solve that problem, look them in the eye and tell them that you would be happy to work with them. Ask them if they would like you to send them an engagement letter. Speak with confidence and strong body language. Then and only then is it okay to advocate for the client to hire you.

If you believe in your ability to do a good job for the client, don't hesitate to tell them. Like the patient in the emergency room, your clients are looking for someone who will take care of them. If you are that lawyer, you are doing them a big favor by telling them.

WHAT ARE YOU GIVING AWAY?

Not everyone is going to become your client. You may not have the right skills, they may not actually need a lawyer, they may not have a good case, or your fee structure may not work for them. Sometimes it is not the right personality fit (for you or for the client).

One way to test the waters is to offer free consultations. Another way is to simply offer free resources like an article or a checklist for a particular type of matter like buying a home. This could be something you do before you engage in a real conversation about the issues they may need help with. That will sometimes cement the relationship and convince the client to hire you.

It is a simple fact of life that humans like to reciprocate. When someone gives you something for free, the natural instinct is to return the favor. One day pre-pandemic, I went to my local tailor/dry cleaner to get a pair of shorts repaired. The hem needed to be resewn, and it wasn't a big job (in fact, it took only two minutes). When I first walked into the shop, the owner must have been downstairs, because no one was behind the counter. I waited a minute or two and then walked out to do a few more chores. I briefly considered going into another shop around the corner, but I have always liked this dry cleaner, and I prefer to do business with them.

When I returned, the shopkeeper took the shorts, fixed the hem, and quickly announced "no charge." I asked three times, "Are you sure?" But the shopkeeper insisted that it was okay. While I am not a big user of dry cleaners or tailoring services (like most of us, I haven't worn full business attire that frequently since the pandemic), I will surely be returning to this shop the next time I have sewing or dry cleaning. Through a small, simple act of generosity, the shopkeeper earned my loyalty.

So what are you doing to earn the loyalty of your clients? What are you giving away to build trust and commitment from potential clients and referral sources?

For me, it's creating content and sharing that with lawyers. My podcast, my blog, my newsletter, the articles I publish, and the speaking I do are all intended to share my wisdom on marketing and career success in the law. My free consultations are designed to provide something of value to a prospect who may (or may not) become a client (but who will remember me when they have a need or meet someone else who does).

In my case, I ask prospective clients to fill out a brief assessment. That forces them to articulate the problem and tests whether they are really committed to solving the problem.

Giving away freebees shouldn't take up all of your valuable time. But in my opinion, it can be an important part of your marketing strategy, especially if you have not worked with the client in the past. If you do enough of this, you'll be like my dry cleaner. You will have earned valuable loyalty that will pay dividends in the future.

One strategy is to charge a small fee for an initial consultation and tell the client that if they decide to work with you, that you will apply the fee to their first invoice. This works particularly well if you offer fixed fees for something like an estate plan. A friend of mine who does estate planning employs this technique.

If it is a client who is a big consumer of legal services, another strategy is to ask the client if they can try you out with a smaller matter.

Selling legal services is a process. Putting pressure on a prospect to hire you can easily backfire, and being a great listener is actually a much more effective way to sell your services. That's good news for lawyers. If you are concerned about coming across as a salesperson and if that conflicts with your identity, know that selling legal services is about providing service. It is about relationships. You can set aside your stereotypes about selling and simply engage in dialogue. Getting the client to articulate their need and their urgency to find a lawyer who can help address the issue is how you will "convince" clients to hire you. While your natural inclination may be to feel a sense of urgency to get the client to sign your retainer agreement, waiting until the prospect articulates a need and their desire to address that need is a better strategy for landing the client.

PART 3

Conventional and Unconventional Advice About Relationship Building

CHAPTER 8
Overcoming a Fear of Networking

For most lawyers, networking is right up there with getting a root canal or spending time in a Porta Potty. It's a necessary and useful activity. But it is not fun.

Many lawyers are introverts and being in social situations can be draining. Attending networking functions can feel uncomfortable. What if you don't know anyone? What should you talk about? How do you find business leads in a large crowd? But networking can help you increase your circle of business relationships. It should be an integral part of your overall marketing and career strategy.

In trying to grow your law practice, the relationships you build today will become the referral sources of tomorrow.

I'm actually a big believer in "retail" relationship building. Having one-on-one meetings with clients, prospective clients, and potential referral sources is a more effective than spending time in a large room where you recognize only a few people. Personally, I spend much more time meeting people for coffee or sitting in on small lunchtime round tables than I do attending large gala events. I enjoy this a lot more and I know it is a much better way to get to know other professionals.

But attending the "right" functions can help you continue to grow your network if you do it right. So it is worth considering whether it is worth carving out some time to attend the bigger gatherings as well.

Here are some tips to help you overcome your natural aversion and get the most from networking events:

- ***Keep your expectations low.*** The goal of attending a networking function is to make a few new connections (i.e., the goal is not to collect as many business cards as possible). If you walk away with two people who you want to follow up with, consider that a success.
- ***Prepare.*** Think about who you might like to meet and think about what you want to say about yourself.
- ***Identify who is attending or who might attend.*** If you have a way of finding out beforehand who is on the guest list, send a LinkedIn request to the people you want to meet and tell them you look forward to seeing them at the event.
- ***Arrive early.*** Look at the name tags or ask to see the registration list and see if you know anyone who is attending. In addition, if you arrive early, it will be easier to connect with people because the room will be less crowded.
- ***Choose events that interest you.*** If there is a speaker, are you interested in learning more about that subject?
- ***Make sure you have prepared a brief introduction which invites questions.*** (Who are you? What do you do? Who do you serve? How do you help your clients?) Introduce yourself in a way that will make people want to find out more about you (i.e., be interesting). Keep it short!
- ***Come with a networking buddy.*** Invite someone who might also be interested and can help you work the room. But don't spend the whole time talking to just them.
- ***Invite others you know.*** Are there clients, referral partners, or colleagues who might be interested? Drop them a note.
- ***If you know the organizer, tell them the types of people you would like to meet at the event.*** Ask the organizer if he or she can make some introductions.
- ***When you approach someone, try to get the other person to introduce themselves first and listen carefully.***
- ***Make good eye contact and ask open-ended questions to get the other person talking.***
- ***Listen for ways that you can be helpful to them*** Is there someone you can introduce them to (at the event or after the event)? Is there an article you can send? Is there a movie, restaurant, book, etc., you can recommend?
- ***Look for odd numbers of people or people who are not already talking to someone else.*** When an even number of people are talking, it is harder to break into the conversation.

- ***Be prepared to answer the question "what's new?"*** If someone you know asks you this question, make sure you have prepared something to say. This can be something personal or professional (e.g., "My youngest child just started high school," "I just came back from a great trip to Utah," "We just won a big victory in Superior Court," "Our firm just merged with an IP boutique firm," etc.).
- ***Try to keep conversations brief.*** If you are genuinely interested in continuing the conversation with someone, ask them if you can follow up for coffee (live or virtual). In answering the question "what's new," just choose one or two things at most.
- ***After the event, make sure to follow up within 24 hours.*** The immediate follow-up can just be to set up a time to talk that might be a few weeks down the road.

You don't have to attend networking functions to be successful with marketing. Personally, I attend events only where I expect to run into a reasonable number of people I already know.

When I do attend events where I know I'll be able to reconnect with a lot of people, I often find that I'm pleasantly surprised. Being at these events gives me a good way to identify some of the people I haven't spoken to in a while. It provides me with an efficient way to stay top of mind with more referral sources.

CHOOSING SMALL GATHERINGS MAY BE A BETTER USE OF YOUR TIME

Every few years, I decide I'm going to attend the annual dinner of one of the charities I support. The event is touted as a great place for lawyers to meet each other, but in truth, it's really a lousy way to meet new lawyers. I go because it provides me with a quick way to shake a lot of hands (i.e., I know a lot of people in the organization, so I see people I already know).

In sharp contrast, I joined a tiny squash and tennis club in my hometown. On the first day I went to work out, I met more new people than I ever do at one of these gala events.

I have nothing against large events. And I think this charity is extremely effective and does good work (and I'll continue to support it). But I don't plan to attend a lot of events like this. It's just not worth my time.

The reason is simple. A large, crowded room filled with a lot of people you do not know is generally not a good environment for relationship building. If your objective in getting involved in nonprofits is to make connections while doing good, aim for committees, projects, or much smaller events where you will actually have the chance to connect with people you want to meet.

To sum it all up, retail networking is much better way to build your network. In one-on-one settings or in very small gatherings, you have more opportunity to have meaningful conversations where you can try and identify ways to be helpful. But if you are invited to an event where you are likely to see some people you already know, you may want to attend. Your conversations may not be that meaningful, but networking functions provide you with an efficient way to reconnect with people. From there you can go retail and set up coffee with two or three people you saw at the event. And it is certainly possible that you will make some new connections as well.

CHECKLIST FOR ATTENDING NETWORKING EVENTS

- ✓ Choose the "right" events
  - ❍ Events where you can interact with clients, potential clients, and referral sources
  - ❍ Events that interest you and where you will feel "reasonably" comfortable
- ✓ Send personalized invites to firm-sponsored events
- ✓ Share notices about external functions
  - ❍ Who in your network might be interested?
- ✓ Review the attendee list prior to the event
  - ❍ It's easier to do if your firm is sponsoring.
  - ❍ Do some research on select registrants or review your notes before the event.
- ✓ Prepare succinct answers to two questions:
  - ❍ What do you do? ("I help . . . " versus "I am an X attorney who does Y." Focus on the problems you solve.)
  - ❍ What's new? (Come with something professional or personal to help start a conversation.)
- ✓ Arrive early and ask to see who is attending
  - ❍ In the alternative, look at the display of name tags.

(continued)

- ✓ Bring business cards
    - ○ If you ask someone for their business card, they'll ask for yours.
- ✓ Come with a networking buddy
    - ○ Plan to work the room together.
- ✓ Look for people standing alone
    - ○ Groups with an odd number of people are easier to break into.
    - ○ Smile and make eye contact.
- ✓ Ask good open-ended questions about them and be a great listener
    - ○ What do you do?
    - ○ What brings you to [name of event]?
    - ○ What's new in your [business/firm/organization/industry]?
    - ○ Ask a question about something you read about their industry/business.
    - ○ Listen for ways that you can be helpful (resources, introductions, etc.).
    - ○ Any vacation/weekend plans? (If it is near a holiday, end of week, etc.)
    - ○ Try to keep conversations to five minutes (ask for permission to follow up after the event).
- ✓ Make introductions
- ✓ Identify 1 to 3 attendees for follow-up
    - ○ Say you'd like to connect after the event.
    - ○ Enter notes into your contact manager.
    - ○ Send a LinkedIn connection.
    - ○ Follow up with something of value (article, an introduction you promised, etc.).
    - ○ Send an email inviting them to coffee, lunch, or Zoom.

BE INTERESTED, BE INTERESTING

In the classic self-help book *How to Win Friends and Influence People*, Dale Carnegie told his readers that they should become "genuinely interested in other people." Nearly 100 years after the publication of that book, the rules of relationship building have not changed, and this still holds true. If you want to make a lasting impression on someone, show that you are interested in them. Listening shows you appreciate them, and appreciation is one of our greatest needs as human beings.

One thing that has changed since the 1930s is that the internet has made researching other people easier than ever. Today, there is no excuse for failing to research someone before you meet them for coffee. LinkedIn, website bios, and general Google searches can tell you a lot about someone's history, about their company, and about their business or industry. It can also give you real clues about their interests and their personal backgrounds.

This is also something you can try to do before attending networking functions. If you have a way of finding out who might be attending, do some research. If the event is sponsored by an organization that lists leadership on its website, check the website and see if there is someone you would like to meet.

But even if you know only a little about the person (e.g., if you are meeting someone for the first time at a networking function), asking good open-ended questions is a great way to get the other person to talk about themselves. So when you are out networking, show some real interest in the other person. Find out what they do, who their clients are, and what they are working on at the moment. Try to extend the conversation beyond business. Find out where they are from, what they like to do on vacation, what movies or music they enjoy, or anything that seems appropriate to discuss.

BEING "INTERESTED" IS THE STARTING POINT

Being "interested" is only half the equation when you are out networking. You also want to be "interesting." And this takes some preparation. When someone asks you "what's new?" you don't want to respond with trite answers like "not much" or "things are busy." Those are conversation stoppers.

You also don't want to launch into a five-minute monologue about a complicated matter that is on your desk.

Take the time to think about what you want the world to know about you... before you head to the function!

Preparation is key. Many lawyers are introverts and are not as comfortable thinking on their feet about what they want to say.

I'm actually an extrovert, but I always try to think of at least one personal and one professional thing to talk about before I go to an event or meet someone for coffee or on Zoom. When I don't do the preparation, I'm often mad at myself afterwards because I find myself stumbling.

Lately, I've been telling people that I'm writing a book or that my middle child is finishing law school soon—that usually triggers a series of follow-up questions. I also talk about the traveling I did this past spring, including nine road trips, which was a dramatic increase for me. Sometimes I mention the men's choir I joined.

It actually doesn't matter that much what you bring up. It doesn't have to be entirely current. There is a long statute of limitations on good news, and it is okay to keep telling people about an award you won or a big case you settled (I would argue that up to a year is fair game, and possibly longer).

As lawyers, we get caught up in analysis paralysis. We are worried about "getting it right," being accurate, or answering the question literally and talking about something that just happened.

In general, there are no right answers to the question "what's new?" You get to choose. Pick something that will engage the curiosity of the other person. If you know something about them, try to choose a topic that you think might interest them. Choose something that is "on brand," and which tells the other person something that is related to your professional interests.

People do like to talk about themselves, and we are all well served by following Dale Carnegie's advice. But taking the time to think about how to answer the question "what's new?" will increase the likelihood that you will get a conversation going. It will also help you find ways to connect with people with whom you are trying to network.

KEEP IT POSITIVE (MOST OF THE TIME)

When sharing what is "new," try to focus on the positive.

Recently, I got together with a business contact who I hadn't seen in a while. I asked her, "What's new?" The first thing she talked about was her new diabetes medication and how it was affecting her mood.

I'm an empathic person, and, naturally, I was happy to give her the space to vent. I felt bad for her and tried to show compassion. But I'm not sure that this is what I would have brought up.

I'm not a big fan of toxic positivity. I do think that venting is very important to our mental health. As lawyers, there is often a lot to vent about. Opposing counsel, clients, and colleagues are not always easy to deal with. In addition, if you are like me, you may be a ruminator who tends to dwell on bad things being reported in the news, "missed" business opportunities, and things going on in your personal life.

I also find it a big turnoff when other professionals go on and on about how successful they are. I know of one coach in particular who seems to like nothing better than to hear herself talk about how great she is.

The truth, however, is that most people are more drawn to the positive. It's not bragging if it is true. And it doesn't cost you anything to be positive.

Leaving out the negative or keeping that part of the conversation to a minimum does not show a lack of integrity.

The bottom line is that you are part of the conversation. While it is great to be interested in others, come to the table with conversation starters.

So try to focus on the positive. It's not that you can't get into personal problems (people do bond around adversity and venting is very important to one's mental health). But try not to lead with this.

WHAT A DEADLY VIRUS TEACHES US ABOUT BUSINESS DEVELOPMENT

Since the pandemic, we have learned a lot about how COVID-19 spreads. While it was hard to see beyond the toll that the pandemic took on our health and on our economy, I already look back nostalgically on this time and remember the months I was able to have dinners with my three adult children, who were all living with us.

I've also realized that the coronavirus has something to teach us about business development and the importance of building a network. In the case of the coronavirus, building that network is clearly a bad thing. In the case of business development, building a network is essential for success.

While COVID-19 spreads from individual to individual, we know that it can spread more quickly when groups of people come together. Also, it can spread exponentially faster when large groups of people are congregated indoors and near each other.

So how is this relevant to business development and business relationship building? The short answer is that it is better to know more people than fewer people. Your referrals will grow more quickly if you know more people and if you deepen your relationship with those people. Referrals will grow even faster if you spend more time with "super spreaders"—the people in your network who like to connect people and who will be ambassadors for your marketing message.

There is some nuance to this. Your contact with any one individual needs to be meaningful. While you may be able to contract the virus if you are in a packed arena and merely coming in contact with one or two infected individuals, spending time at large networking events alone won't necessarily build your network. Follow-up is critical. Getting to know a lot of people very superficially won't necessarily help "spread" your marketing message. Going deeper is important.

That is another one of the silver linings I have discovered at this time. During the pandemic, and even now, people are looking for ways to connect, and they are more open. I'm finding that I'm getting to know people on a more personal level (Jim plays guitar; Molly is a grandmother; Dan has a mother-in-law who just died of cancer in an assisted living facility). Zoom can give us a window into the lives of our colleagues, clients, and professional contacts.

Look for the people who are ready, willing, and able to take your message and spread it "virally." Your reputation will grow more quickly. While networking is a volume business, it is a volume business only up to a point. There is no way to develop deep relationships with thousands of people.

The mantra of my business networking group ProVisors is *Know, Like, Trust, Refer*. If you want your business to grow, get to know a reasonable number of professionals who may be in the position to refer matters your way. Spend additional time cultivating relationships with the super spreaders (the people who will carry your message to others), and be careful about spending too much time at very large events where your interactions will at best be fleeting. Most importantly, be healthy, and the next time we are in a pandemic, practice safe social distancing!

CHAPTER 9

Do Live Conferences Still Matter?

In-personification

[in-per-son-uh-fi-kay-shuhn]

noun

taking a virtual relationship to the next level by meeting in person

EXAMPLE OF IN-PERSONIFICATION USED IN A SENTENCE

Jane and Michael finally met up offline for the first time last week, and it did not go well. They simply weren't ready for in-personification!

Neologism courtesy of Dr. Ezra Keshet, Associate Professor of Linguistics, University of Michigan
Inspiration to create the word: Matthew Cahill, CEO, The Percipio Company

In April of 2024, I attended the Annual Education Conference of the National Association for Law Placement (NALP). It was my first live conference since the start of the pandemic. It had been over two years since I returned to live events; but this was really the first large multi-day event I had attended in over five years. And I had a great time!

Since 2020, a lot of my networking activity has been virtual. I know that many people have grown weary of using Zoom, but for me, virtual meetings have been a game changer. My network has grown dramatically in size, quality, and—most importantly—geographically.

A key reason for this is that ProVisors, my business networking group, did a terrific job of migrating to a virtual platform at the very start of the pandemic.

Since the organization has meetings all over the country, this shift enabled me to dramatically increase my business network in many other cities, including New York, DC, Atlanta, Dallas, the Bay Area, Chicago, and Los Angeles, to name a few.

In fact, I actually wasn't sure whether I really needed to go to live conferences anymore. While I do speak locally at live bar association events from time to time, it wasn't clear to me that I would get a lot of value from traveling a great distance, including taking the time to fly somewhere and incurring the expense.

It turns out that I was wrong.

The NALP conference was held in Boston, so I actually did not have to travel. I was representing the ABA Career Center board. But I was also an active participant in some of the workshops, and I spent a considerable amount of time in the exhibit hall meeting other vendors who serve the legal community.

What was striking to me was the quality of the interactions that I had. I found myself very energized by being in seminars where I had the chance to interact with other people in a more spontaneous way. I felt more connected to the people I met, and there were a lot more serendipitous interactions with directors of professional development at law firms and internal and agency recruiters (i.e., good referral sources for my coaching business, and potential clients as well).

Something else happened at that conference that really changed my perspective. I had arranged to meet a friend/consultant who flew in from San Francisco. While we were eating lunch, the Director of Learning and Development at an AmLaw100 firm walked by. She was a former client of my friend, and my friend made an introduction. We spoke a little about the coaching. Three days after the conference ended, I was in discussions another colleague of the director about a new coaching program that was being set up by the firm.

None of this would've happened if I had not attended this conference.

A month later, I attended another conference in Omaha, this time, co-sponsored by several divisions of the American Bar Association. I was there for a meeting of the ABA Career Center board, but I also attended a number of great workshops as well. And I met some of the people that I have been working with through the ABA, including members of another board, which approved this book's publication.

Attending conferences is, of course, not for everyone, and for the more introverted lawyer, it may feel more intimidating than a small committee meeting of a bar association, trade association, or nonprofit organization. But the tips I supplied in the previous chapter on networking functions can help you to navigate conferences like this.

And if you choose the right conferences where you can meet the prospective clients and referral sources that you want to meet, then these could be high-value activities.

One way to navigate a conference is to volunteer to be a presenter. Being a thought leader can get you some visibility at a conference. It is also a way to feel more comfortable with your role at the conference. It provides you with a more organic way to connect with other professionals.

Another way to get value from a conference is to connect with the speakers.

At each conference I attended, I made an effort to introduce myself to some of the speakers. I found that they were very receptive to connecting with me, and I ended up with a significant number of follow-up meetings after both conferences.

Virtual events are here to stay. If you attend virtual events that provide breakout groups for real connection, that can be a great way to leverage your marketing time without having to leave your office or home. But live events can provide an opportunity for higher-quality connection. The trick is to get the right balance that works for you.

CHAPTER 10

Want to Grow Your Network Faster? Try Taking Notes

Since the start of the pandemic, my network has grown exponentially. Much of that has to do with my involvement in the ProVisors business network. Simply put, it's the best organization I've ever joined! I've met great people, some of whom have become referral partners, and others are professionals from whom I've learned a tremendous amount (about marketing, coaching, leadership, and a host of other subjects).

While I always tell my clients that the quality of your relationships is more important than quantity, it does feel good to have a really strong network nationally. Zoom and other virtual tools have enabled me to attend many more networking functions since the start of the pandemic.

But as I continue to meet new people, quite honestly, it can be challenging to keep track of all of the details.

While I might remember what they do professionally, knowing things that are more personal is critical in relationship building. Who likes small dogs? Who is a basketball fanatic? Who likes to drink fine wines? Who is interested in the outdoors? Who grew up on Long Island like me? Who likes classical jazz? These may seem like unimportant details when you're trying to do business, but in many ways, personal information is very important in building your network.

So here is what I do. I write things down! I do this either while I am on a Zoom call or on a phone call. But even if you just want to focus on the conversation, or if you meet somebody in person, all you need to do is make sure to write down some notes after the meeting ends or after you walk out of the event.

If people hand you a business card, that gives you one place to keep the information until you have a chance to record it. The important thing is to do it soon so that you don't forget.

While I know that some lawyers are doing this already, in speaking to hundreds of attorneys in the last 30 years, I know that many are not.

Having some sort of contact manager is also essential. There are many solutions on the market, but Outlook is actually just fine if you're just working by yourself. A fancier CRM system is nice, but it is useless if you are not capturing information in it.

The important thing is to find a way to write things down so that you can go back to them, and so that you can remember who to send that funny cartoon to or who you can share that article with.

As a lawyer, you know how to do this. You are certainly generating notes about your clients, meetings, witnesses, experts, deal terms, or anything else related to your representation.

No one likes to take the time to do this. Tracking time, documenting what you have done, and making a point of deciding on next steps before the day ends are all cumbersome.

But when it comes to relationship building, documenting is an invaluable activity that can help you greatly as you cultivate relationships over time. So make it a habit.

These details are also important when you reconnect with people so that you can reestablish rapport. I take notes on what we discussed when I have a virtual one-on-one or a live coffee.

As we preach at ProVisors, people refer work to people they know, like, and trust. That trust does not grow simply by sharing with each other what our technical skills are. It runs much deeper. In fact, there is a good argument to be made that we often have no way of knowing whether another professional is good at what they do. But if we know what they do, if we like them, and if we trust them, we infer the rest.

The information you learn about your potential referral sources helps build that trust, and if people in your network trust you and if you stay top of mind over a long period of time, it will greatly increase your chances of generating referrals.

Sample Address Book Entry

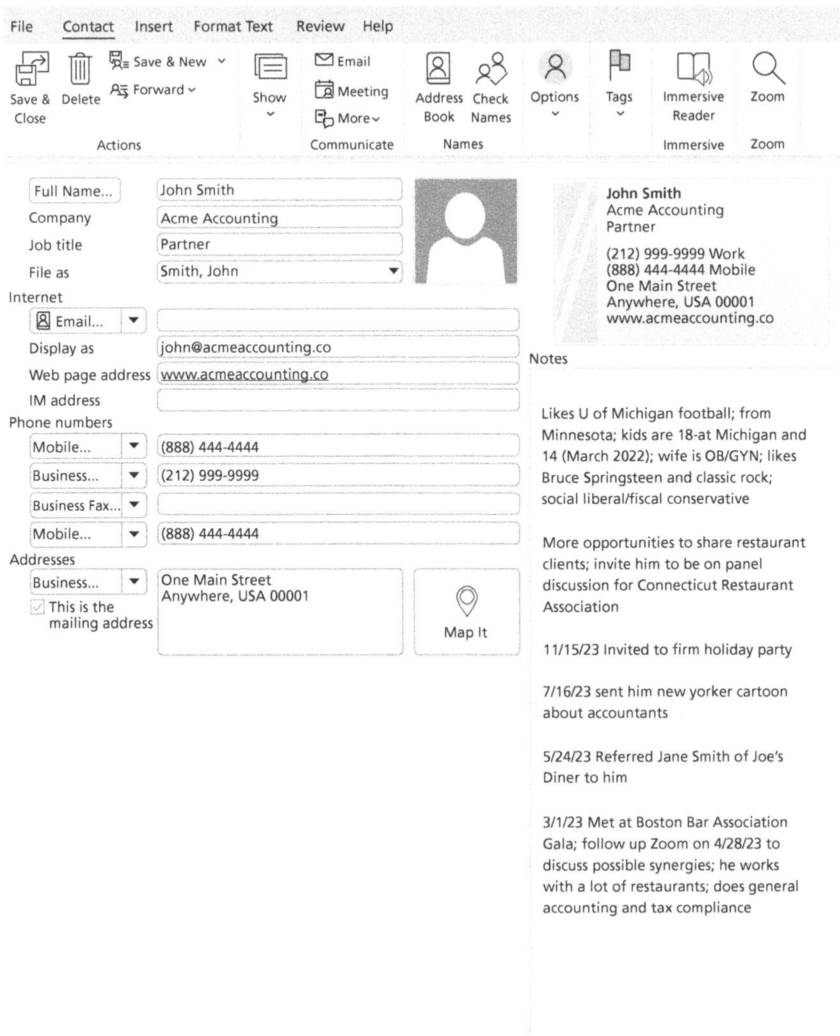

WHAT INFORMATION SHOULD YOU BE GATHERING ABOUT THE PEOPLE IN YOUR NETWORK? CHATGPT PROVIDES SOME SUGGESTIONS

I am always telling my clients to learn what they can about the people they meet. What you learn can be very helpful in staying top of mind. In the last section, we discussed the importance of taking notes. But what notes should you be taking?

I sat down to create a checklist that my clients could refer to. I opened a Word document and started typing. Pretty quickly, I realized that this was a great job for AI.

What follows is a dialogue I had with ChatGPT.

This section is intended to educate you about the types of information you could be learning about people in your network. But it is also intended to show the tremendous power of using ChatGPT for idea generation. These are only suggestions about the types of professional and personal information that are helpful to learn. This is not a checklist of every piece of information you need to know. You should pick and choose appropriately.

ChatGPT is like a very good intern! If you give it the right instructions, you may end up with a pretty good work product. But you need to check the work. Although in this case, I had to ask follow-up prompts to get what I wanted, what follows is verbatim!

Stephen Seckler (SES): I'm writing an article about ways to build business relationships. I would like to share ideas that will be practical and helpful. One of the things I want to focus on are the types of information that it is useful to learn about people in your network so that you can build your relationship with them. I would also like you to indicate for each item why it is useful to know that fact about the person and what one can do to build the relationship using that information.

ChatGPT: *Building strong business relationships is crucial for professional success. Here's a list of key information types to learn about people in your network, along with reasons why they're useful and strategies for leveraging this information to strengthen your relationships:*

1. *Professional Background*
   Why Useful: *Understanding someone's professional journey, including their current role, past experiences, and future aspirations, helps you appreciate their skills, experiences, and goals.*
   How to Use: *Share opportunities, advice, or connections that align with their career path. Engaging in discussions about industry trends relevant to their background can also be beneficial.*

(continued)

2. *Educational Background*
   Why Useful: *Knowing their educational background can provide insights into their expertise and interests.*
   How to Use: *Connect on common educational experiences or subjects of interest. This can also guide you in recommending relevant professional development resources or events.*

3. *Personal Interests and Hobbies*
   Why Useful: *Personal interests give a more holistic view of the person beyond their professional life.*
   How to Use: *Engage in conversations about these interests. If you share a hobby, this can be a great way to bond. You can also recommend articles, events, or groups related to their hobbies.*

4. *Work Challenges and Needs*
   Why Useful: *Understanding the challenges they face at work helps in providing targeted support or solutions.*
   How to Use: *Offer advice, share resources, or connect them with others who can help in addressing these challenges.*

5. *Cultural Background*
   Why Useful: *This helps in understanding their perspectives and may inform their professional interactions.*
   How to Use: *Show respect and interest in their cultural background. This can include celebrating cultural events with them or understanding their communication style.*

6. *Personal Achievements*
   Why Useful: *Acknowledging their achievements shows appreciation for their hard work and success.*
   How to Use: *Congratulate them on their successes, both in formal settings and casually. This can also lead to discussions about their journey towards these achievements.*

(continued)

7. *Professional Goals and Aspirations*
   Why Useful: *Knowing what they aspire to achieve can help you align your interactions and support toward these goals.*
   How to Use: *Share resources, introduce them to people in your network, or advise them on steps that can help them reach their goals.*

8. *Communication Preferences*
   Why Useful: *Everyone has different communication styles and preferences, and understanding these can make interactions more effective.*
   How to Use: *Adapt to their preferred style of communication, whether it's emails, calls, or in-person meetings. This shows respect for their comfort and can lead to more productive exchanges.*

9. *Industry Insights*
   Why Useful: *They might have unique insights into specific industry trends or changes.*
   How to Use: *Engage them in conversations about these insights. This not only shows that you value their opinion but can also provide valuable information for your own professional knowledge.*

10. *Networking Preferences*
    Why Useful: *Understanding how they prefer to network (events, one-on-one meetings, online platforms) can help in building a relationship in a way that's comfortable for them.*
    How to Use: *Invite them to networking events they prefer or engage with them on platforms where they are most active.*
    By focusing on these aspects, your business relationships can become more meaningful and beneficial. Remember, the key is not just to know these details but to use them thoughtfully to foster genuine connections.

(continued)

SES: What about values and beliefs, personal challenges, work and personal anniversaries, and career milestones?

ChatGPT: *Including values and beliefs, personal challenges, work and personal anniversaries, and career milestones in your understanding of someone in your business network can significantly deepen the relationship. Here's how these elements are useful and ways to utilize this information:*

1. *Values and Beliefs*
   Why Useful: *Knowing someone's core values and beliefs can help you understand their decision-making process and what drives them.*
   How to Use: *Respect and acknowledge their values in your interactions. This can involve supporting causes important to them or engaging in projects that align with these values.*

2. *Personal Challenges*
   Why Useful: *Being aware of personal challenges they might be facing shows empathy and understanding.*
   How to Use: *Offer support or accommodations that might help them. Sometimes, just being a good listener can be invaluable.*

3. *Work and Personal Anniversaries*
   Why Useful: *Remembering anniversaries such as the start of their business or a personal milestone like a wedding anniversary shows attentiveness and personal care.*
   How to Use: *Send them a note or message acknowledging these anniversaries. If appropriate, a small gift or gesture can also be meaningful.*

4. *Career Milestones*
   Why Useful: *Career milestones are significant achievements in one's professional journey.*

(continued)

How to Use: *Celebrate their milestones, whether it's a promotion, completion of a big project, or a work anniversary. Acknowledging these achievements can strengthen your professional bond.*

By paying attention to these more personal and significant aspects of someone's life, you demonstrate a deeper level of care and interest that goes beyond mere professional courtesy. This can lead to stronger, more resilient business relationships built on mutual respect and understanding. Remember to approach these topics with sensitivity and discretion, as they can be quite personal.

SES: Can you add to the list more personal facts like marital status, children, preferred types of music, favorite movies, or books, places where they vacation? Also, please list some of the hobbies that you mentioned above and expand on that as well as in sports, theater, music, or other general interests that are not actually hobbies, including politics or civic engagement.

ChatGPT: *Certainly! Adding more personal facts to your understanding of someone's profile can greatly enrich your business relationships. Here's an expanded list that includes these aspects, along with reasons for their importance and how you can use this information:*

1. *Marital Status*

   Why Useful: *Knowing their marital status can offer context for their life outside of work.*

   How to Use: *Respect boundaries and engage in appropriate conversations, possibly including their spouse in certain social invitations.*

2. *Children*

   Why Useful: *Understanding their family structure can offer insights into their priorities and time commitments.*

   How to Use: *Show interest by asking about their children's well-being and activities in a respectful manner. Share relevant family-friendly resources or events.*

3. *Preferred Types of Music*

   Why Useful: *Music preferences can reveal aspects of their personality and provide a common ground for conversation.*

   How to Use: *Discuss music, share recommendations, or even invite them to concerts or musical events.*

(continued)

4. *Favorite Movies or Books*
   Why Useful: *Favorite movies or books can be a great conversation starter and offer insight into their interests.*
   How to Use: *Discuss these favorites, suggest similar titles, or even gift a book or movie you think they'd enjoy.*

5. *Vacation Preferences*
   Why Useful: *Knowing their preferred vacation spots can reveal a lot about their interests and relaxation style.*
   How to Use: *Engage in conversations about travel, share experiences, or offer recommendations.*

6. *Hobbies*
   Sports: *Engage in conversations about their favorite sports, share news, or even attend games together.*
   Theater: *Discuss recent plays or musicals, recommend shows, or plan a group outing to a theater.*
   Music: *Talk about their favorite genres or artists, and share experiences related to music events or performances.*
   Art: *Engage in discussions about art forms they like, visit galleries together, or share information about art exhibitions.*

7. *General Interests*
   Politics: *If they are open to discussing politics, engage in respectful and informed conversations about current events.*
   Civic Engagement: *Discuss community projects, volunteer opportunities, or civic issues they are passionate about.*
   Each of these pieces of information offers a unique opportunity to connect on a more personal level. The key is to approach these topics with sensitivity and respect, ensuring that your interest is genuine and not intrusive. By doing so, you can create a more meaningful and lasting business relationship.

SES: Please expand on actions I can take like sending items of interest to people like articles or cartoons. Also, what are events or activities that I can use to build my relationship understanding people's personal interests?

(continued)

ChatGPT: *Expanding on your actions to build relationships through sharing interests and organizing events or activities, you can create more engaging and personal connections. Here are some specific actions and ideas:*

1. *Sending Articles, Cartoons, or Videos*
   Action: *If you come across an article, cartoon, or video that aligns with their interests or is relevant to a recent conversation, share it with them via email or social media.*
   Impact: *This shows you're thinking of them and value their interests, which can be a great conversation starter or a way to stay in touch.*

2. *Book or Movie Recommendations*
   Action: *Based on their favorite genres or recent discussions, recommend books or movies. You could even start a casual book or movie club with a few contacts.*
   Impact: *Sharing media can lead to deeper discussions and shared experiences, fostering a sense of community.*

3. *Invitations to Sports Events*
   Action: *If they are interested in a particular sport, invite them to a game or watch a match together at a sports bar or a viewing party.*
   Impact: *Sharing a sports experience can be a fun way to bond and show that you value their interests.*

4. *Theater, Concerts, or Art Exhibitions*
   Action: *For those interested in the arts, invite them to a play, concert, or art exhibition. This could also include virtual events.*
   Impact: *Cultural outings offer a sophisticated and enjoyable way to connect, allowing for shared experiences and discussions.*

5. *Golf Outings or Other Sporting Activities*
   Action: *Organize or invite them to a golf outing, a friendly game of tennis, or other sporting activities.*
   Impact: *Participating in sports together can foster camaraderie and offer a relaxed environment for conversation.*

(continued)

6. *Cooking Classes or Wine Tastings*
   Action: *Invite them to join a cooking class or a wine tasting event, especially if they have expressed an interest in culinary experiences.*
   Impact: *Such activities are enjoyable and provide a casual setting for engaging conversations.*

7. *Travel and Adventure Activities*
   Action: *If they enjoy travel, discuss potential destinations or share your experiences. You might even organize a group travel event or a local adventure.*
   Impact: *Sharing travel stories or experiences can create lasting memories and deepen connections.*

8. *Charity Events or Volunteer Work*
   Action: *If they are involved in civic engagement, participate in a charity event or volunteer activity together.*
   Impact: *Engaging in community service can bond you over shared values and a sense of purpose.*

9. *Networking Events or Professional Workshops*
   Action: *Invite them to relevant networking events, workshops, or seminars. This is especially effective for contacts who are keen on professional development.*
   Impact: *Such events provide opportunities for learning and meeting new people, which can be mutually beneficial.*

10. *Personalized Gifts or Notes*
    Action: *On special occasions or milestones, send personalized gifts or handwritten notes that reflect their interests or achievements.*
    Impact: *Personalized gestures show thoughtfulness and appreciation for the relationship.*
    These actions and activities are effective ways to build relationships because they demonstrate genuine interest and investment in the other person's personal and professional well-being. Always ensure that your actions are considerate and appropriate for the nature of your relationship with each individual.

(continued)

SES: Are there any caveats that you would offer about which activities to choose beyond knowing what are someone else's interests? What about my own interests? Should that be a factor? Can you include in this a discussion of authenticity?

ChatGPT: *Absolutely, while aligning activities with someone else's interests is important, there are several caveats and considerations to keep in mind, including your own interests and the importance of authenticity. Let's delve into these aspects:*

Choosing Activities: *Beyond Knowing Interests*

1. *Consider Mutual Enjoyment*
   While it's crucial to consider the other person's interests, your own enjoyment is equally important. Engaging in an activity that you genuinely enjoy can lead to more authentic interactions and shared enthusiasm.

2. *Balance Professionalism and Personal Interests*
   In a business context, it's important to maintain a professional demeanor. Ensure that the activities are appropriate and do not compromise professional boundaries.

3. *Respect Comfort Zones*
   Some activities, while enjoyable for one, might be out of the comfort zone for another. It's important to choose activities that both parties are comfortable with.

4. *Be Mindful of Time Commitments*
   Consider the time commitment required for the activity. Busy professionals might appreciate more concise, less time-consuming engagements.

5. *Cultural Sensitivity*
   Be culturally sensitive in your choice of activities. What might be a common activity in one culture could be inappropriate or misunderstood in another.

Factoring in Your Own Interests

1. *Shared Interests for Authentic Connections*
   Engaging in activities that align with both your and the other person's interests fosters a more authentic connection. Shared passions or hobbies can be powerful bonding tools.

(continued)

2. *Avoid Forced Interests*
   Participating in an activity you have no real interest in can come across as disingenuous. Authenticity in business relationships is key to building trust and rapport.

3. *Finding Common Ground*
   If your interests don't align perfectly, find a middle ground where both parties can enjoy the experience. This could be trying something new to both of you.

The Role of Authenticity

1. *Authenticity Builds Trust*
   Genuine interactions are the foundation of any strong relationship. People are more likely to engage and invest in relationships where they feel a sense of sincerity and honesty.

2. *Avoid Overreaching*
   While it's important to show interest in the other person's likes and dislikes, avoid overreaching or pretending to be someone you're not. Authenticity involves being true to your own character and values.

3. *Consistency is Key*
   Ensure that your actions and the way you present yourself are consistent over time. Inconsistencies can lead to distrust or a sense of unreliability.

4. *Transparency and Openness*
   Be open about your intentions and transparent in your interactions. If an activity or topic is outside your scope, it's okay to admit it. This can actually lead to more genuine and meaningful conversations.
   In summary, while aligning activities with someone else's interests is crucial in building business relationships, incorporating your own interests and maintaining authenticity are just as important. Relationships built on mutual enjoyment, respect, and authenticity are likely to be more rewarding and sustainable in the long run.

SES: We can gather a lot of this information by speaking with our business network, but what are some other ways to gather this information (e.g., social media, Google searches)?

(continued)

ChatGPT: *Gathering information about your business network can indeed go beyond direct conversations. Here are some alternative methods:*

1. *Social Media Platforms:*
   Platforms like LinkedIn, Twitter, Facebook, and Instagram can provide a wealth of information about professional backgrounds, interests, and personal milestones.
   LinkedIn is particularly useful for professional details, while other platforms may offer insights into personal interests and activities.

2. *Google Searches:*
   A simple Google search can yield articles, interviews, or news mentions that reveal professional achievements, interests, and public appearances.
   This can also include finding any blogs or personal websites they might have.

3. *Company Websites:*
   If they are associated with a particular organization, the company's website often has bios of key personnel, detailing their professional background and sometimes personal interests.

4. *Industry Publications and Newsletters:*
   Subscribing to industry-specific publications can provide insights into their professional accomplishments and viewpoints, especially if they contribute articles or are mentioned.

5. *Networking Events and Conferences:*
   Attend industry events, conferences, and seminars where they participate. These can provide insights into their professional interests and expertise.
   Observing their interactions and topics of discussions can also offer valuable information.

6. *Mutual Contacts:*
   Mutual professional contacts can sometimes provide insights, especially regarding professional interests and networking preferences.
   However, it's important to approach this method with discretion to maintain privacy and professionalism.

(continued)

7. *Public Records and Articles:*
   Public records (where accessible and appropriate) can provide information on business ventures, published work, and sometimes civic engagement. Articles in which they're featured can provide both professional and personal insights.

8. *Alumni Networks and Publications:*
   If you share an alma mater, alumni networks and publications can be a good source of information about their educational background and achievements.

9. *Volunteer Organizations and Nonprofits:*
   If they are involved in volunteer work or nonprofits, these organizations' websites and publications can reveal their interests in civic engagement and values.

10. *Professional Directories and Associations:*
    Membership in professional associations can indicate areas of professional interest and expertise.
    Some associations publish member directories or profiles.

11. *Podcasts or Webinars:*
    If they have participated in podcasts or webinars, these can be excellent sources of information about their professional opinions, achievements, and sometimes personal interests.

12. *Book and Article Authorship:*
    If they have written books or articles, these works can offer deep insights into their professional expertise and personal passions.
    When using these methods, it's crucial to respect privacy and ethical boundaries. The goal is to gain a better understanding to foster genuine professional relationships, not to intrude into personal lives without consent.

The following checklist is a summary of the points made by ChatGPT.

RELATIONSHIP BUILDER CHECKLIST

1. **Professional Background**
   Know their current role, past experiences, and aspirations. This helps you align your interactions and offer relevant opportunities.
2. **Educational Background**
   Understand where they went to school and what they studied. This can guide discussions or professional development recommendations.
3. **Personal Interests and Hobbies**
   Knowing hobbies gives a fuller picture of the person and allows for conversations beyond work.
4. **Work Challenges and Needs**
   Understanding their work struggles helps you offer tailored support or connect them with resources.
5. **Personal Challenges and Needs**
   Understanding their personal challenges (sick family member, aging parents, illness, etc.) gives you good reasons to follow up and offer help, sympathy, or simply show that you care enough to ask how things are going with X.
6. **Cultural and Religious Background**
   Awareness of their cultural or religious background informs respectful interactions and deeper understanding. Understanding what holidays they may observe provides opportunities to send well wishes.
7. **Personal Achievements**
   Acknowledge milestones like awards or completed projects. This builds rapport through recognition.
8. **Professional Goals and Aspirations**
   Knowing where they want to go professionally allows you to offer relevant advice or introductions.
9. **Communication Preferences**
   Adapt to their preferred method of communication, whether email, phone, or in-person, for smoother interactions.
10. **Industry Insights**
    Be aware of their views on industry trends. Engaging in these conversations shows respect for their expertise.
11. **Networking Preferences**
    Some people prefer large events; others prefer one-on-one meetings. Tailor your invitations accordingly.

(continued)

12. **Marital Status & Children**
    Understanding family dynamics offers insight into their priorities and allows for personal, respectful conversations. Knowing what is happening with their children and other family members provides opportunities for follow-up.
13. **Preferred Music, Movies, Books**
    Engage with them over shared media interests, deepening personal connections.
14. **Vacation Preferences**
    Travel preferences reveal relaxation styles and can lead to engaging discussions or trip recommendations.
15. **Sports, Theater, Art**
    Shared interests in these areas can form the basis for social engagements and deeper bonds.
16. **Civic Engagement & Politics**
    Respectfully engaging in their civic or political interests can strengthen your relationship if approached appropriately.

Where to Get Information

1. **Be an Active Listener**
   Ask good questions and demonstrate that you are eager to understand their situation and really get to know them as a person.
2. **Social Media Platforms (LinkedIn, Instagram, Facebook)**
   Review profiles for professional and personal insights.
3. **Google Searches**
   Look up news articles, interviews, and blog posts.
4. **Company Websites**
   Read bios for professional details.
5. **Mutual Contacts**
   Discreetly gather insights from shared acquaintances.
6. **Industry Publications**
   Check contributions or mentions in professional newsletters.
7. **Public Records & Articles**
   Use publicly available information about their business ventures or achievements.
8. **Alumni Networks**
   Tap into shared educational institutions for insights.

(continued)

Caveats

1. **Respect Boundaries**
   Avoid intrusive questions about personal matters unless they voluntarily share.
2. **Be Authentic**
   Engage in activities that both of you genuinely enjoy. Avoid faking interest to appear agreeable.
3. **Time Sensitivity**
   Busy professionals appreciate concise interactions—don't ask for too much time unless necessary.
4. **Cultural Sensitivity**
   Be mindful of cultural differences in communication and relationship building.
5. **Privacy**
   Use only publicly available or shared information. Don't overreach into their private lives.

CHAPTER 11
Building Your Business Relationships with Politics, Religion, and Humor

"I refuse to join any club that would have me as a member."

—*Groucho Marx*

I've come to realize over the years that when I find something in common with another individual, it is easier to build rapport. Sometimes that thing is professional (we do similar work, we have similar clients, we are interested in the same subject matter, etc.). But more often, the thing we have in common is more personal in nature.

I connect well with people who enjoy the same music (classic rock, folk rock), the same hobbies (playing guitar, playing squash or other racquet sports), the same movies (stories about dysfunctional families, parody, documentaries), the outdoors, the same podcasts (*The Daily*, *Stay Tuned with Preet*, *Fresh Air*, *Hidden Brain*, *Freakonomics*, *The Happiness Lab*), etc. While I'm not that interested in organized sports, I do genuinely enjoy speaking with individuals who are passionate about sports. We'll talk more about that in chapter 13.

Are there any interests I don't mix with business? Conventional wisdom says that religion and politics are bad topics to bring up with people you don't already know. Humor is also risky when you are trying to cultivate business relationships. For the risk averse attorney, these are topics best left alone in a business setting.

With some significant caveats, I disagree.

TRIBALISM AND NETWORKING

As human beings, we are all fundamentally tribal. We like to belong, and we like to identify with groups that we belong to. Looking for these connections should be a conscious part of your efforts to build your professional network. In addition, we are wired to trust people who are "like" us.

For example, be on the lookout for:

- Alumni of your high school, college, or law school
- Fellow sports fans (e.g., Red Sox Nation—need I say more?)
- People who live in the same community
- Individuals who have worked for the same company
- Individuals who grew up in the same place
- People who have played the same sport
- People who vacation in the same place
- The parents of your children's friends
- People with the same musical tastes or dislikes (e.g., how do you feel about Beyoncé?)
- Where you went to camp (or where your kids went to camp)
- People who share your hobbies

And what if you have the same religious upbringing or share a common set of political beliefs?

RELIGION AND POLITICS

Religion and politics create some of the strongest ties between people. The challenge is how to bring up these topics without offending. For the risk averse attorney, politics and religion are particularly fraught.

In my case, I live in a pretty liberal part of the country, so it's not that risky to make a disparaging comment about the 45th president. But if I don't know someone well, I usually give them an opening by bringing up the topic in a relatively neutral way and listen for their reaction. For example, in early 2022, I said to some new people in my network, "I heard that the January 6 Commission is going to start holding public hearings." If anyone had called it a witch hunt, I would have moved on.

Also, by just being a good listener, people will often give you clues about their political beliefs. If you ask a lot of open-ended questions when you meet someone (think direct examination), you can learn a lot about them and then decide how to proceed.

The intersection of religion and politics is particularly fraught. For example, I have a strong Jewish identity. But I am extra careful with my views on the Israeli-Palestinian conflict, especially since the start of the war in Gaza (although if I know someone shares my views on the subject—which are actually very nuanced—that is a strong bond that ties us).

Religion and politics are highly emotional, and that is why they are great sources of identity for most of us. Unfortunately, we are living in a country with a lot of polarization. But when we can establish (in a safe way) that someone shares our belief system, we have a bond that goes even further than rooting for the same sports team (although that can be like a religion), graduating from the same law school, growing up in the same town, or liking the same music. We can use this polarization to our benefit.

Finding shared experiences, interests, or beliefs makes the conversation flow. It increases our feeling of being connected to someone, and ultimately it increases the likelihood that we will like and trust that individual (and vice versa). Sharing common political or religious beliefs can greatly increase that likelihood.

In fact, there is one theory that organized religion developed as humans moved from nomadic existence where everyone knew each other to cities where you couldn't know everyone. Being part of the same religious faith and practice was one way to know that someone was trustworthy.

Bernie Madoff is a great example of using this human tendency in an evil manner. Bernie Madoff's Jewish identity did help him connect with and build trust among many Jewish clients, particularly within the tight-knit Jewish community, where he leveraged his reputation and social connections to attract investments. This trust was a significant factor in the success of his Ponzi scheme, as it enabled him to access a network of wealthy and influential individuals who believed in his legitimacy.

Obviously, I'm not suggesting that Bernie Madoff is a role model for leveraging your religious identity to advance your business interests. But we can clearly learn some lessons from Madoff about how religious identity can build trust.

HUMOR

I've saved humor for last, but humor is one of my greatest interests. I love parody. I love sharing cartoons and memes with people in my network. My list of all-time *great* movies and TV shows includes *Dodgeball*, *This Is Spinal Tap*, *Bridesmaids*, *The Hangover*, *Talladega Nights*, *Borat*, *Best in Show*, *Wayne's World* (my first date with my wife), *The Big Lebowski*, *Groundhog Day*, *Monty Python's Life of Brian* (religious parody!), *The Office*, and *Curb Your Enthusiasm*, to name a few. I frequently quote these movies and shows when I'm talking to my clients and my business contacts.

Earlier this year, a client told me he hired me because he heard me speaking on a podcast about how I like to write parody lyrics. He liked my advertisement for Verizon (*Sign Up Now for Verizon*—sung to the tune of Bruce Springsteen's title cut *The Rising*, his homage to 9/11 and New York).

When I get a coaching prospect laughing, I generally know that is a good sign. But humor can really backfire, especially on Zoom. It is also important to consider how your attempt at humor will be received. I already noted that in chapter 5 where I mentioned a failed attempt at humor during a webinar I was presenting.

I would argue that most lawyers could probably use more humor, not less. Our fear of offending someone can provide a good censor for inappropriate comments.

BEING YOUR AUTHENTIC SELF

If you try to use religion, politics, and humor in your business networking, you are bound to offend someone along the way. At the same time, you'll find people who want to work with you and spend time with you because they can see you are not afraid to be authentic. But be particularly careful on virtual platforms where it is hard to read facial cues and gauge reactions.

You are paid as a lawyer to be a trusted advisor. If you want to engender trust, be your authentic self. If sharing your political or religious views is a turnoff to some prospects, you'll make it up by finding the clients who really appreciate you. Similarly, if you can figure out an appropriate way to use humor to connect, you'll be laughing all the way to the bank!

A NOTE ABOUT EMBRACING DIVERSITY, EQUITY, AND INCLUSION

While finding common ground such as shared beliefs or interests can be foundational in establishing rapport, it is equally important to value and embrace differences. A diverse workplace, where various ethnic, religious, and cultural backgrounds are represented, fosters creativity, innovation, and resilience. By prioritizing diversity, equity, and inclusion (DEI), we ensure that our client base reflects the diversity of the world around us. Engaging with people who bring different perspectives and experiences enriches our professional interactions.

This inclusivity not only strengthens our relationships but also enhances our ability to serve a broader and more varied clientele effectively. Thus, while we may seek out similarities to connect on a personal level, recognizing and celebrating our differences makes our professional networks more robust and dynamic.

At the same time, despite our religious and political differences, we can still find common ground through shared interests, experiences, and a similar sense of humor. These connections allow us to bond and build meaningful relationships across diverse backgrounds.

CHAPTER 12

Monetizing Your Children and Pets to Grow Your Law Practice

"If you want a friend in Washington, get a dog."

—*Harry S. Truman*

In the winter of 2022, my wife and I had a "guest dog" staying with us. We were once proud dog owners. But that ended in 2017, just before our last child went off to college and our 14-year-old yellow Lab died. (Question: *When does life begin in the Jewish tradition?* Answer: *When the dog dies and the kids go off to college.*)

At the time, we were actually living in my mother-in-law's apartment in Brookline, Massachusetts, while we were doing some home renovations. It's a much more urban environment than our home in Newton, and after several months, we still didn't know many of the neighbors.

In the five days that Buttons was with us (yes, that's the name of the adorable Australian Labradoodle that we hosted), I spoke to more people than I had in five months. I met people in the park whom I would never have spoken to. We had several occasions to chat. I spoke to people in the elevator I had never met.

It was a great reminder that dogs are a very effective social lubricant.

If Buttons were still with us ("who's a good boy?"), I know that I would begin to cultivate relationships with other dog owners (or just dog lovers). And maybe some of them would turn out to be lawyers who need my help, or lawyers or other professionals who know lawyers who are frustrated with their marketing, with their careers, or want to develop better leadership skills.

I'm actually not that big a dog lover, and when we had Chutney, our yellow Lab, I wouldn't say that she was a big source of social connection for me. Where Chutney made a difference, however, was when I was standing on the sidelines watching my kids play soccer or dropping my kids off at play dates with Chutney in tow.

For me, having kids was a great way to cultivate business relationships.

In fact, some of my best clients ended up being the parents of my kids' friends.

There are many ways to be successful in building a law practice. Fundamentally, it is important to choose activities that you enjoy and that feel authentic. And it is important to choose activities that give you the opportunity to build relationships with potential clients and referral sources.

If you happen to have children and you show up at a lot of their activities or if you have a dog and you spend time at dog parks, these are powerful tools in your marketing arsenal that are just waiting to be activated.

Relationship building is really at the core of business development success. So, finding authentic and enjoyable ways to build relationships with prospective clients and referral sources is really the key.

I'm not suggesting that you go to dog parks or hang out at youth sports only looking for opportunities to hand out your business cards. Quite the contrary. Go to the Little League game and enjoy watching your kids play. Sit in the audience at the dance recital and clap as loud as you can! But make the effort to talk to other parents. Find out what they do. Listen for ways that you can be helpful to them. If and when the time seems right, see if you can find an opportunity to get together with them (i.e., on another day) to talk business. Same with trips to the dog park.

I have clients I met when our kids were in middle school. It wasn't until they were in high school that I actually began doing some marketing and career coaching with them. I focused on getting to know them on the sidelines, at school events, and at social gatherings. I didn't pitch. Over time, we got to know, like, and trust each other, and eventually, that turned into paying work.

I worked with a trusts and estates lawyer who has two adorable young children and a cute Boston terrier. Her target market is "developing net worth" families (i.e., professionals just like her who are just starting a family—and maybe have a pet!). I encouraged her to go to the dog park and get to know people in the neighborhood. That has helped her grow her practice.

If you participate in kid activities or hang out at dog parks simply trying to pitch your services, that is sure to backfire. When you are selling legal services, you are selling trust. Going right for the "kill" is no way to build trust.

But if you genuinely enjoy watching your kids play youth sports and perform at recitals, or if you enjoy seeing your dog and someone else's dog chase the same ball, then don't miss the chance to have conversations with the parents (of the kids and/or of the dogs). It's an organic way to grow your network, and it's highly effective as long as you give it time!

CHAPTER 13

If You Don't Like Sports, Try Becoming a "Sports Fan Fan"

If you live in a city like Boston, it's pretty hard to ignore what is going on with the sports scene. During the time that my kids were growing up, the Boston Red Sox and the New England Patriots won many championships. In 2024, the Boston Celtics regained their glory.

Because of the sports culture of the city, sports does tend to be a popular topic in networking situations. But if you're like me, sports viewing does not occupy a significant portion of your free time. I tune in when one of our teams makes it to the championship round, and I may enjoy one night every few years at Fenway Park, although I'm just as likely to end up at Fenway to hear a concert featuring aging rockers (I saw the Who a few summers ago—it was inspiring to see that Pete Townsend can still twirl his arm while playing guitar and not end up in the hospital).

Sports does tend to be a topic of great interest to many of the people in my business networks, and despite my general disinterest in spending a few hours watching baseball, football, or any other sport, for that matter, I have never found that to be a hindrance in getting to know other professionals. In fact, while I am not that interested in spending time watching sports, I'm perfectly happy to hear what others have to say about our teams. In other words, I consider myself a *sports fan fan*.

The advantage of being a sports fan fan is that you don't have to be emotionally invested in the outcomes and experience the disappointments that come inevitably during most seasons. In Boston, it's also a lot cheaper than buying a ticket. And it frees up a lot of time for other pursuits (both personal and professional).

On the other hand, it is nice to be informed, and I would have to say that I greatly enjoy meeting somebody who is very enthusiastic about sports. I might say "some game last night!" and then I basically let them do all the talking. It's an efficient way to get up to speed on the latest trends, injuries, and upset victories, and losses.

The truth is that being interested in other people is a very good way to connect with them. The basic idea is that you want to be interesting and have something to talk about (your own personal interests/hobbies/vacations/movies you've seen; a case you are working on; interesting developments in your practice area). But it is even more important to be interested in other people. Dale Carnegie wrote about this almost a century ago in *How to Win Friends and Influence People* (become generally interested in other people).

This means that when I'm trying to connect with people at networking events, I show interest in them first. If they have a professional interest or expertise, I'm happy to ask questions about that. If they seem interested in talking about sports or some other hobby/interest I don't share, I ask a lot of questions to learn more. Some people I meet are interested in world travel. Others are very interested in music and still others are interested in the outdoors, skiing, biking, or dogs. You don't have to be interested in what they are interested in, in order to show appreciation, and since your interest in connecting with them. We discussed this in chapter 8.

Of course if you do share a common interest with somebody, then you have more natural ways to connect with them over time. But in terms of just keeping the conversation going, your initial connection could be around something that is more interesting to them.

CHAPTER 14

When It Comes to Business Development, Monogamy Is Not the Best Policy

A while back, I was talking to a coaching client about a prospect he had been courting for the last two years. The prospect, Dave (not his real name), does high-end real estate deals. My client, John (not his real name), is a commercial real estate lawyer who does sophisticated real estate lending work.

John and Dave get along well. John has taken Dave to a number of basketball games, and they enjoy spending time together. More recently, Dave introduced John to two of his friends—a real estate developer and an accountant—whom John has also invited to games. The four of them have also gone out to dinner.

John has interviewed Dave for a Q&A series he published through his law firm's newsletter, and he even invited Dave to be on a recent real estate industry panel that was sponsored by his firm.

While John has never gotten any work from Dave, it is clear that Dave is looking for the opportunity to send deals to John. He respects John, and he likes the fact that John works for a top firm. John also sees the potential to get referrals from the accountant and work for his partners from the real estate developer.

But in February, Dave told John that he is joining another real estate investment company. The general counsel of the new company has a law firm he already uses. One of the key partners at that law firm was a former law firm partner of the general counsel. Dave told John that, for now, he would be unable to send legal work to John.

John was, of course, disappointed. This could have been a $500,000-a-year client. But clearly, that was not going to happen anytime soon.

Shortly after John got the news, he told me that he had tickets to an NBA playoff game, and he wanted to know if he should invite Dave. While I had been encouraging John to do everything he can to nurture the relationship with Dave, at this point I told John that it was time to move on and focus on other prospects.

It is certainly possible that someday Dave will be able to give deals to John (either because his general counsel sees value in bringing in other law firms, the general counsel moves on, or because Dave moves on to yet another real estate investment company). And John should absolutely keep in contact with Dave. But his level of contact with Dave should slow down. He needs to pursue other leads and move Dave to the B-list (i.e., check in with him maybe twice a year).

John invited someone else to the game.

PERSISTENCE IS KEY (WITHIN REASON), BUT SUCCESS IN BUSINESS REQUIRES DIVERSIFICATION

Relationship building does require some persistence. But there is a balance between being persistent and stepping over the line. At the same time, it is important to understand that many of the business relationships that you cultivate will never lead to actual business. You need to keep your volume of contacts high if you want to be successful. We'll say more about that in Part 4.

When you are selling legal services, the goal is to develop relationships with potential clients and referral sources who get to know, like, and trust you. That trust takes time to build. More importantly, legal services by their nature are not needed every day. You need to be in front of your prospects and referral sources over time because it is hard to know when the need will arise. This is why when it comes to marketing, it is important to put in check your sense of urgency about everything (a quality that many lawyers share).

So, focusing on just a couple of prospects is not a great strategy.

In baseball, batting.300 (getting a hit three out of ten times at bat) means you are a superstar. Venture capitalists are happy if they "hit it out of the park" with one in ten investments. (They expect to lose money one-third of the time, break even one-third of the time, and more than make up for that with the remaining investments—but in many cases, only one of those investments will generate significant returns.)

Similarly, if you have a prospective client or what you think could be a great referral source, don't put all your eggs in one basket. Diversify your "investments." You don't know which ones will produce results.

Sometimes, you'll have very unexpected wins and get business that didn't seem likely. Sometimes you'll put in a lot of effort, get a lot of buying signals from a prospect, and, like my client John, the client goes another way because of things that are out of your control.

FOCUS ON ACTIVITY, NOT ON RESULTS

Of course, it can be very dispiriting when you don't land business, especially when the relationship seems to be building and the prospect seems interested. Dr. Larry Richard's research tells us that compared to the general population, lawyers rank low on resilience and don't like what they perceive as failure. But frequently, the time is just not right either because the need isn't there or the client doesn't have the ability to hire you. Over time, that can change.

For example, another client of mine (I'll call her Anne) is an IP lawyer who is very good at keeping up with relationships over time. She just landed one of her largest clients ever. The general counsel who hired Anne was an associate she had worked with 15 years prior. When that associate went in-house, he was unable to send work to Anne. It was a big company that already had well-established relationships with outside counsel. During those 15 years, Anne would check in with him periodically. Occasionally, she would invite him to be on panels. Eventually, it paid off.

Anne does this with dozens of prospects. In fact, every week she makes a habit of having coffee or talking on the phone with a few prospects in her network. The goal is simply to build the relationship and find ways to be helpful. "Helpful" can be in the professional sense, but even recommending a good movie, contractor, or vacation spot is a way to be helpful.

Some prospects eventually send her work. Some never will. Most of the time, it has little to do with Anne.

What Anne understands is that building a practice is a volume business. The more "at bats" she gets, the more likely it is that she will be successful. She focuses on the "at bats."

When thinking about building your network, you want to go deep, but you also want to go wide.

KEEPING YOUR LEVEL OF ACTIVITY HIGH TAKES OFF THE PRESSURE

In building your law practice, you don't want to take every client that walks in the door. Having the ability to say no to a prospective client who doesn't really fit into your wheelhouse (or who is likely to be difficult to work with) is important. If you have more in your pipeline, you can be a little choosier. Of course, this is easier as you get further along in your career.

You'll be less dispirited by the opportunities that don't work out. And you'll build a stronger network in the end. While monogamy may be the best policy in marriage, it's not a good strategy for career or marketing success.

GO FOR DEEP RELATIONSHIP BUILDING, DON'T JUST COLLECT BUSINESS CARDS

In this chapter, I've tried to underscore the importance of diversifying your relationship building. You don't want to put all of your eggs into one basket.

At the same time, when it comes to business relationships, quality is more important than quantity. If all you do is add names to your contact manager and you don't do anything to nurture those relationships, you aren't really doing business development. Having thousands of connections on LinkedIn is of minimal value if you aren't doing more to deepen those connections.

If deepening your connection with people in your business network seems daunting, keep reading. For much of the remainder of this book, we will be focusing on just that: how to build solid relationships with clients, potential clients, and referral sources.

PART 4

Act Like a Venture Capitalist and Other Miscellaneous Advice

CHAPTER 15

Persistence, Follow-Up, and Avoiding Fatal Attraction: Tips for Building Your Network

"I sent an email a week ago to a former client who moved to another company. I didn't get any response. Do I send another email message? How long should I wait? What should I say?"

"I met a potential referral source at a networking event last fall. We spoke by Zoom two weeks later, had a nice conversation, and then nothing happened. When should I contact her again?"

Effective follow-up is an issue that I work on with almost every client I meet. Whether I am coaching lawyers who are trying to build their practice, counseling lawyers on their next career move, or helping lawyers to develop better leadership skills, follow-up is something we always discuss.

If you want to be successful in your legal care, it is important to develop great legal skills. But being a great technician is insufficient. Building a strong professional network is just as important. Communicating effectively with your colleagues is critical. And if you want to build your network, persistence and follow-up are essential.

Despite your follow-up, you will fail a lot more than you succeed. Act like a venture capitalist and understand that most of your investments in business relationships will not produce returns. But know that maybe 5 percent of the time, you will achieve a lot of success and that will make up for the misses. And some of the "misses" will eventually become successes.

RESPOND TO EMAILS WITHIN A REASONABLE AMOUNT OF TIME

I've always made a habit of responding to email messages within a day (even if just to say I'm sorry but I'm busy right now and will try to get back to you next week—or something like that). While I don't always live up to this standard, I believe it is common courtesy to acknowledge that someone is trying to communicate with me (unless they are simply trying to sell me something).

While I consider responding to emails in a timely fashion the professional thing to do, I recognize that some of the people I am trying to reach are overwhelmed and simply don't have the bandwidth to respond.

AUTO REPLIES CAN HELP MANAGE EXPECTATIONS

Many lawyers make effective use of auto replies to deal with this problem. They set the expectations, so the sender at least knows the message was received. If you do use an auto reply, a best practice in my opinion is to give the sender the name of someone whom they can reach out to if their matter is time sensitive. Some lawyers I know—generally more senior attorneys, who are more old-school—have an administrative assistant monitoring their account so that time-sensitive matters are addressed quickly.

More often, I find that people in my network who are busy simply don't respond at all.

Even knowing that many professionals are simply too busy to respond, it is hard not to take it personally when someone ignores you. But there are many reasons why emails you send may get no response.

For starters, email has been proliferating at an exponential rate since it became the dominant form of business communication in the late 1990s. The sheer volume of email that most professionals receive in a day is daunting, and it is only growing.

It is also important to remember that there are many other reasons why you may not be getting a response when you email someone.

And it is important not to go negative when you haven't heard from someone.

SPAM FILTERS ARE A PROBLEM

Spam filters are becoming a lot more aggressive in weeding out unwanted solicitations from our inboxes. It is incumbent on each of us to check our spam folder daily. I've been seeing more and more legitimate email ending up there.

There is also "user error" at play. In the old days, when you sent a letter, you had a physical envelope that went in the mail. With email, however, failing to click Send or to cc the right person means the message won't get delivered, and you may never know it.

In addition, sometimes people have things going on in their personal lives that make it hard for them to respond.

I've had every one of these things happen multiple times in the last few months. I sent a message that the recipient didn't see because he was too busy. I've had recipients who saw a message I sent and forgot to get back to me because they were involved in too many things, and my message moved down the queue. Many messages I've sent have landed in spam folders. Some of my recipients thought they had hit Send but hadn't, or they replied to the person I wanted them to meet but forgot to cc me. This past year, two people told me that they were dealing with a death in the family and had been out of pocket for a few weeks. They had not set up an auto reply.

GETTING PAST SPAM FILTERS AND PERSISTING

So what are the best ways to address these challenges? Here is my list:

- If you don't get a response, don't be afraid to send a follow-up email a couple days later asking if the person received your first message. I resend the message with a "cover message" saying: "Just making sure you received my message."
- If the follow-up gets no response, try texting or calling a few days later. You can leave a voicemail message saying, "Making sure you got my email message" or "Just making sure my message didn't end up in your spam folder."
- Unless your matter is time sensitive, wait a few days between follow-ups so you don't appear too aggressive. As lawyers, we tend to have a sense of urgency about everything. When it comes to relationship building, it is important to keep that sense of urgency in check.
- If you have reached out a couple times and there is still no response (and it is a relationship you really want to cultivate), wait a couple months, and

then send the individual something of value (an article on a subject that might interest them or a recommendation about something they might like personally; being a good listener will give you clues about that).

- Each time you reach out, try to change your message a little and, if possible, say at least one new thing (so you don't sound like a broken record). If you actually sent them a proposal at any point, try the phrase "Let me know if you need anything else from me."

When you are doing your outreach, try to keep your emails very simple. People are busy, and while we are very good as lawyers at capturing detail, no one wants to read an email message that goes on for several paragraphs. In addition, try to limit the content of each email to one or two things. Don't go with the "everything but the kitchen sink" approach. Send two separate emails if there are two different things to follow up on.

Most of the time when I do this, the person on the other end apologizes. In the past several months, I've received four messages from lawyers who were either embarrassed that they hadn't responded, thankful that I told them to check their spam folder, or apologetic for their own "user error."

FOLLOWING UP IS HARD FOR LAWYERS

For many lawyers, following up like this is not intuitive or comfortable. Most of us went to law school thinking that we could work hard, deliver great service, and the work or the job offers would follow.

In fact, many of us are reluctant to do this kind of follow-up because we don't want to come across like a salesperson. Being persistent feels aggressive and salesy (and maybe even unprofessional).

We also shy away from follow-up because we are afraid of rejection.

And not only is it easy to take it personally when we don't hear back, sometimes we will infer ill intent or bad character on the part of the other person (they don't want to hear from us or they are too self-absorbed to respond to us). Of course, this is simply the fundamental attribution error at play. It is hard to know what someone else's intentions are just by observing their behavior.

In truth, this really just means we are being narcissistic. Someone else's lack of follow-through likely has nothing to do with us.

If you are trying to build your practice, follow-up is crucial. Legal services are generally big-ticket items that people don't need all the time. If you want prospective clients and referral sources to think of you when a problem arises, you need to be visible over time. One phone call or one email message will not create the ongoing visibility you need.

If you are worried about being rejected when you send an email asking to meet for coffee or by Zoom, you can try a technique employed by a coaching colleague of mine, Amy Gardner. Amy keeps a whiteboard in her office. On the whiteboard it says: *Emails sent without catastrophe*. She will add hash marks for every email sent regardless of whether the other person responded. Needless to say, the number of emails send "with catastrophe" is generally zero for her clients.

Is it possible to overdo it with your outreach? Of course. Sending the same email message five times in a month will not reflect well on you. But in my experience, this is rarely the problem. Just the other day, a client of mine reached out to a few law school classmates who were now in corporate roles (i.e., prospective clients). He hadn't spoken to them since graduation, which was more than ten years ago. But as I reminded him, it's never too late to renew your college ties.

If you have any questions about how you can make your own communications more effective, particularly if they are more in the realm of marketing communications, please email me. I check my spam folder daily! And I promise to get back to you within 24 hours (unless I'm on vacation, in which case, you will get an auto reply).

PROBABLE CAUSE IS THE STANDARD FOR FOLLOW-UP IN NETWORKING

Last year, I was doing a workshop on business development for a client. One of the participants was the managing partner, who asked me, "What is the most common issue you work on with your clients?"

I thought briefly about the question, and then I realized that there was an obvious answer: follow-up. As I've said, the issue of follow-up is relevant in all my coaching work, not just in the coaching I do on business development.

In marketing, staying top of mind over time is crucial. Follow-up ensures that potential clients and referral sources will think of you when an opportunity presents itself.

Follow-up is also crucial for anyone doing career exploration. Employers like to hire professionals who are interested in their firm or company. Good follow-up demonstrates your interest.

We've noted that in business development, the "right" career opportunity doesn't come along every day. If you want people in your network to keep thinking of you as they become aware of firms and companies with hiring needs, then following up over time is important.

Finally, good leaders must find appropriate ways to follow up with their team to make sure everyone is on the same page and feeling motivated to do their best. Follow-up highlights who on your team may be hitting some stumbling blocks. It gives you a chance to ensure that members of your team are focusing on the "right" tasks. Follow-up also demonstrates that you are invested in their success.

LAWYERS DO NOT LIKE REJECTION

Because this is such an important point (and a lifelong struggle for me), let me underscore again that as a group, we don't like rejection. When we don't hear back from a potential client (i.e., after having a promising initial consultation), we assume this person is not interested in working with us.

If an accountant who serves clients in the same industry has canceled lunch, we assume the accountant is not interested in building a referral relationship.

If we have interviewed with another firm or company and we don't hear back, we assume that the employer has found another candidate. Rather than taking the opportunity to demonstrate our continued interest, we assume the worst.

Our natural tendency as lawyers (by disposition and by training) is to analyze. We often overthink things.

ROME WASN'T BUILT IN A DAY; NEITHER ARE RELATIONSHIPS

Humans are not purely rational beings. When it comes to relationships and relationship building, it is important to allow things to build organically. Our analytical tendencies can interfere with our efforts to build rapport. We need to allow time for relationships to build. That requires follow-up.

The truth is, there are many reasons why people cancel appointments or fail to respond. Perhaps they are busy. Maybe your email ended up in their spam folder. Or maybe there was a death in the family, or they are sick.

The key is to assume nothing when you haven't gotten a response. Acknowledge your feelings of rejection, and then act anyway!

So, how much certainty do you need to decide that you should follow up?

THE BAR FOR FOLLOW-UP SHOULD BE LOW

In my opinion, the bar should be low when deciding whether you should follow up with a potential client, referral source, employer, or direct report. Unless you have a solid reason to believe the other individual isn't interested in connecting, your default should be to follow up.

That's true whether you are trying to build your law practice, trying to advance your career, or trying to develop your team.

To put it in legal terms, don't look for clear and convincing evidence, proof beyond a reasonable doubt, or even a preponderance of the evidence. Don't think you need to get past summary judgment on the issue before you decide to act.

All you need is probable cause.

According to ChatGPT:

> *Probable cause exists when there is a reasonable basis to believe that a crime has been committed and that the person accused may have committed it. It is a relatively low standard of proof, requiring more than mere suspicion but not as much evidence as would be required to prove guilt beyond a reasonable doubt.*

The same goes for deciding whether you should follow up with someone. If there is probable cause to think that it might be worth reaching out a few more times, don't wait for proof beyond a reasonable doubt.

CHAPTER 16

Finding C.H.I.L.L. Referral Partners to Increase Your Referrals

My three adult children all attended a private middle school. We actually live in a community that is well known for its high-quality public schools. In fact, all three of them attended our public elementary school. They even graduated from our public high school, but my wife and I were concerned that middle school was the weak link. Instead, we opted for much smaller class sizes and an inclusive culture that we thought would be beneficial to each of them.

We have no real way of knowing how things might have turned out if they had gone to the public middle school. There are no do-overs in raising your kids. From an educational perspective, though, we feel that we got our money's worth.

As it turns out, there were some other benefits of being part of this community.

While there were plenty of other middle-class families like us at the school, we were also introduced to many families with tremendous wealth. These were the 1 percenters who are well-connected in law, business, the life sciences, financial services, and many other industries.

In theory, it was great for my business to meet these parents. Over time, some of these relationships did bear fruit. I met a number of parents who eventually became my clients, and I did generate some referrals.

But during our six-year run at the school, I actually generated a lot more business outside of the rarefied world of private school. Despite the fact that many of these parents were well-connected and had great networks, getting to know them better was not a priority for me. I was not motivated to deepen our relationship.

By the time our last child headed back to our public high school, I had reached the conclusion that meeting people who are well positioned to help you does not mean that they will want to help you or that relationships with them are ones you want to cultivate. Authentic relationship building requires more.

RELATIONSHIP BUILDING IS KEY IN MARKETING AND IN CAREER ADVANCEMENT

I speak all the time with my clients about the importance of building authentic relationships. Relationships are important for career advancement and for building your business. Being good at what you do will only get you so far. No one achieves success on their own.

But how do you decide where to focus your energy? How do you know what relationships to build?

Your time is a limited resource. Spending time on activities that are unlikely to have a short-term benefit is particularly challenging when you have plenty of billable work to do. And whether you are working for other lawyers or trying to build your own practice, you want to be strategic in deciding how to manage the time you spend on relationship building.

I have come up with an acronym to help you be more strategic in your relationship building. The acronym is C.H.I.L.L. You can use C.H.I.L.L. to triage those relationships that are worth cultivating and those relationships that look good on paper but are less likely to help you build your practice.

Before I get to that, I want to say just a little more about relationship building. While I am focusing here on identifying the types of people who can be helpful to you, an important part of relationship building is finding ways that you can be helpful to others. And just because you don't see an obvious way for someone to be helpful to you in the short run, I am not trying to suggest that you should avoid or ignore those people altogether. Sometimes it's just nice to be a helpful person. Also, there is a Jewish expression: *You never know when you will meet your wife or your wife's sister*.

SO, WHO ARE C.H.I.L.L. REFERRAL PARTNERS?

C.H.I.L.L. stands for Capacity, Helpful, Integrity, Likeable, and Low-Hanging Fruit.

People who are C.H.I.L.L. have:

- **Capacity** to help
- A **Helpful** mindset
- **Integrity**
- They are **Likeable**
- And the best place to start is with the **Low-Hanging Fruit**

Know Your Ideal Client and Who Has the Capacity to Make Referrals

In thinking about where to focus your networking energy, the starting point should always be figuring out who is your ideal client. If you know what kinds of clients you are trying to serve and who are the other professionals who work with the same clients, then you can be much more focused on seeking out the *right* people to connect with.

For example, if you focus on handling business disputes between partners of closely held businesses, then corporate lawyers who represent these types of businesses may have the capacity to refer work to you. This is true especially if there is no one in their firm who is a litigator.

Similarly, accountants who do tax work and general corporate accounting for similar businesses are good referral partners.

If you focus on domestic relations, then therapists may be good referral sources.

Not Everyone Has a Helping Mindset

Knowing that someone has the capacity to be helpful is a good starting point. But not everyone *is* helpful.

I have met a lot of recruiters over the years. In fact, I was a recruiter for more than two decades. I know that recruiters are speaking all the time to lawyers they can't place. I know they are frequently speaking to law firm leaders who want to develop their talent. Recruiters have the capacity to refer to me work that they don't do. I have the capacity to refer to them candidates and employers for legal searches.

But not every recruiter I meet has a helpful mindset. Some are singularly focused on connecting with lawyers they can place right now or legal employers who have an immediate need to find talent. Meeting other professionals is not a priority for them. I learned this the hard way by trying to cultivate a relationship with a recruiter who ended every conversation with "Sorry, Steve, I have to take this" (and "this" was always some hot candidate or "valued" law firm client—i.e., not me).

So, I focus on those recruiters who want to be helpful to the lawyers they can't place. Those are the recruiters who take the long view. I spend my time with recruiters who genuinely enjoy making referrals and who ask the right questions that might elicit a need I can fulfill.

I Is for Integrity

The *I* in the acronym stands for integrity. You may identify people who have the capacity to help you and who have a helpful mindset. Despite this, some people never follow through on anything.

If somebody wants to help, but they never do what they say they're going to do, maybe they aren't the best people to spend time with.

Similarly, if you're trying to build relationships with other professionals who serve the same industry, focus on those professionals who you think will be trustworthy enough to do a good job for your clients. You want to make referrals to professionals with integrity.

The First L Stands for Likeable

Are these individuals whom you connect with organically? Do you like them? Do they share your values?

In my example, when my kids were in middle school, I did meet some parents who shared my interests and whom I genuinely liked. But there were definitely some who seemed to be in a position to help me but who did not share my values. Cultivating those relationships did not feel authentic. So, I learned quickly not to invest a lot of time and energy getting to know them even if my kids were friendly with their kids.

Start with the Low-Hanging Fruit

The best people to cultivate relationships with are the people whom you already have a strong relationship with. These are your friends, former classmates, people who belong to the same church or synagogue, family members, former colleagues, former clients, or existing clients who are happy with the services that you are providing.

These are the people who already know, like, and trust you. These are the people who can really help you build up your network the most quickly and on whom it will be easiest for you to focus your energy.

STICK WITH C.H.I.L.L. PROFESSIONALS OVER TIME

If you focus on building authentic relationships with professionals who have both the capacity to help and a helpful mindset, you are more likely to generate referrals. If you connect with the people you like and who do what they say they are going to do, you will end up with more inbound traffic.

Just remember that staying top of mind over time is crucial in generating referrals. So, find ways to keep your connections warm and start with the low-hanging fruit. They are the people who are most committed to your success.

JUST SAY NO

Sometimes, you will be on the receiving end of people wanting to connect. As you grow your network, your contacts will make introductions, and more people will find you through LinkedIn. While it is nice to have inbound requests, once again remember that your time is limited. You want to engage with C.H.I.L.L. referral partners.

Many of us receive LinkedIn requests from people we don't know. While some of those could be good people to engage with, here are some red flags to watch out for:

- The person is primarily interested in selling you a product or service rather than in building a genuine professional relationship.
- The request is from someone with a questionable reputation and involves activities that could compromise your integrity.

- The person is asking you to help them before you know them.
- You have previously interacted with the person and had a negative experience.

If someone in your network makes an introduction and you are not interested in meeting with that person, it is okay to say no. Setting boundaries is a critical part of effective time management. Depending on your relationship with the person who made the introduction, you should still thank that person and let them know who a better introduction might be.

Of course, if the introduction was made by an important client or referral source, you may want to have the meeting anyway.

EMBRACING COOPETITION

As lawyers, we can be a competitive lot. We want to win our cases or get the best deal for our clients. Our clients hire us to be zealous advocates. We want to be selected when clients are interviewing more than one law firm.

But keep in mind that the lawyers on the other side of your matters could someday become great referral sources.

For starters, you may exclusively handle plaintiff's matters. If lawyers who do only defense work receive an inquiry about a plaintiff's matter, they need to refer that to another lawyer. If you maintain a professional relationship with defense counsel, perhaps they will think of you for these referrals.

Similarly, a type of matter may be too small or too big for another lawyer. Your fees may be more in line with what a potential client can pay. And conflicts of interest can be a big source of referrals from other lawyers.

Depending on your practice area, building relationships with attorneys who do similar things is often a good use of your time. In fact inviting your competitors to serve on panels with you or engage in other joint marketing can also be worthwhile.

As lawyers, we often see other attorneys as the competition. In reality, a healthy dose of *coopetition* can help you generate significant work.

I appear on a lot of panels with other coaches. I've had many appear as guests on my podcast *Counsel to Counsel*, and I've even coauthored articles with some of my competitors. At times, I have been able to refer coaching work to other coaches who have different areas of expertise. I have also been on the receiving end of referrals from coaches when they had an inquiry from someone who had a need that was not in their wheelhouse.

Be a good lawyer for your clients. But don't ignore relationships with counsel on the other side of your cases. If they see you as a good lawyer and they respect you, that respect could keep you top of mind when they need to send work elsewhere.

USE A ONE-PAGER TO HELP MAKE AN INTRODUCTION

If you want to make it easier for your C.H.I.L.L. referral partners to send you referrals, it can be helpful to come up with language they can use to make an introduction. You can also create a separate one-pager that also describes the types of problems you solve and the kinds of clients you help. Personally, I like the idea of having a separate PDF or Word document so that the person you are sending it to has some place to file it.

Here is an example some language that a client of mine came up with. Referral sources can simply cut and paste this when they are making an introduction for him.

Here's how to introduce Jason Lawyer to someone in your network:

> *I'm writing to introduce you to a great IP litigator that I know who is looking to expand his network with manufacturing companies: Jason Lawyer.*
>
> *Jason is a trial lawyer who helps his clients protects their technology. He also defends their freedom to use it. He is looking to meet executives at manufacturing companies so he can better understand how they are using patents, trademarks, and trade secrets.*
>
> *Jason has lots of great war stories about all things intellectual property, and I think you would enjoy meeting him. Check out his bio and his list of publications where you can read more about him. He can be reached by phone at 617.666.6666 or by email at* Jason.Lawyer@Lawfirm.com.

INTRODUCTIONS ARE JUST AS VALUABLE AS REFERRALS

Asking another professional for introductions or referrals may feel uncomfortable to you. As lawyers, we don't like to come across as salesy and we don't want to invite rejection.

Here is the reframe: how do you feel when the people you like ask for introductions? In all likelihood, you enjoy being helpful and you are happy to connect people you like. Other people feel the same way.

More importantly, while referrals are ultimately what you are trying to generate, people in your network are much more likely to be able to make introductions than to send you referrals. If you are specific in your ask about who you want to meet, you will make it easier for the other person.

Are you looking to meet accountants and bankers who work with restaurants? Are therapists a good source of referrals for divorce matters? Are realtors or commercial brokers a good source of real estate deals? Are you looking to meet owners of small service businesses? C suite executives at technology companies? When you are out building your network, asking for referrals is fine. But the people you meet are much more likely to know other professionals who work with the same clients you serve regardless of whether they have an identified legal need.

Over time, referrals will come to you (and you will be able to make referrals). But the opportunity to refer work to another professional is something that doesn't happen every day.

In order to make that happen, you need to stay top of mind over an extended period of time. In the next section, we will address ways for you to do that.

KEEPING TRACK OF YOUR NETWORKING ACTIVITY

If you are consistent with your networking activity, it is easy to lose track of when to connect and with whom. One strategy is to create a spreadsheet with your most important contacts. On the next page is a sample of a spreadsheet I use.

I always recommend that my clients keep some notes on this master networking list. But I also emphasize that it is better to keep a lot of the details about an individual in your contact manager. Similarly, while a master networking list is a great way to have a master dashboard for tracking your networking activity, setting reminders in your calendar or putting reminder flags on your emails is a great way to remember to circle back to someone in a few months.[1]

[1] For an electronic version of this spreadsheet, please reach out to steve@seckler.com

Master Networking List

Attorneys

Name	Affiliation	Where did we meet?	Notes	Next Steps

Clients
(past, present,
and potential)

Name	Affiliation	Where did we meet?	Notes	Next Steps

Referral Partners

Name	Affiliation	Where did we meet?	Notes	Next Steps

Other

Name	Affiliation	Where did we meet?	Notes	Next Steps

CHAPTER 17

Be a "Quarterback" for All Your Clients' Professional Needs (Business and Personal)

Giving referrals is one of the best ways to get referrals. It is human nature to want to reciprocate. If you send business to one of your referral sources, you increase the chances that they will send work back to you.

Of course, it is important to choose your referral sources strategically. We discussed that in chapter 16.

Giving referrals is also a great way to build your relationships with your clients and with other people in your network. It shows that you are a resourceful person who can be helpful in many ways beyond your own area of expertise.

Yana Feldman has a great system for increasing the number of referrals that she is able to give. Yana is a trusts and estates lawyer in New York who tries to "quarterback" all of her clients' legal needs (i.e., even if they go far beyond her area of competence). She makes a point of telling her clients about her large network and encourages her clients to think of her not just as a trusts and estates (T&E) lawyer but also as a well-connected lawyer who knows a lot of other professionals and can make introductions.

I met Yana through my business networking group, ProVisors, and I have to agree with her. Those of us who are part of the ProVisors network have access to several thousand lawyers and other professionals who we can introduce.

If your existing clients continue to see you as a resource when a matter is finished, they are more likely to reach out to you in the future.

To sum it all up, be like Saul Goodman in *Breaking Bad* (or *Better Call Saul*). He brands himself as a well-connected attorney who can make many introductions that his clients need. (*I know a guy who knows a guy… who knows a guy.*)

If you know the show *Breaking Bad*, you know that there are a lot of ways you should NOT emulate Saul Goodman (unless you want to end up in jail, or worse). But demonstrating that you are a resourceful attorney will go a long way in helping you build your practice. People will come to you with all of their professional problems. That means that one of three things can happen:

- You stay top of mind with that individual, and they come to you when they do need your services or know of someone who does.
- You get to make referrals to other professionals in your network, and that reinforces your relationship with those professionals.
- You feel good about being helpful (and less like a salesperson).

GIVING JUST ONE REFERRAL MAY BE THE BEST OPTION

When someone is looking for a referral, how many choices should you provide? Is choice always a good thing? Not in my opinion, especially when it comes to referrals.

I was in the supermarket several months ago and, when I turned up the snack aisle, I saw a mother deeply involved in a negotiation with her two young children. Apparently, one child likes Cheetos and the other likes Fritos. Neither of them like Doritos. The multi-pack that the mother had grabbed off the shelf had all three.

It was a classic sibling fight, and I'm glad I'm long past those days of parenting. From my vantage point, the whole scene was hilarious. I suspect the mother didn't feel the same way.

Going to an American supermarket can actually be overwhelming at times. Most of us have an abundance of choice when we go shopping, and it is actually hard to choose between five different varieties of peanut butter. In fact, stores like Trader Joes and Costco play off this. They offer far less variety in most product categories.

So what does this have to do with referrals?

When someone asks us for a referral, they are looking for someone to solve their problem. They are asking us either because they don't know anyone with that expertise or they have no way of assessing who is good at that thing.

If you give someone three names to contact, you are not really making it easier for them to decide who to hire. A better approach is to find out as much as you can about the issue they are trying to solve, and then suggest to them who you think is best given the situation. Tell them that they can come back to you if they need another name (e.g., if the person wasn't a good fit).

Giving referrals is a great relationship-building tool. It strengthens your relationship with the person who needs the referral, and it strengthens your relationship with the person who receives the referral (and who might refer back to you).

Obviously, you don't want to give a bad referral. But helping someone find a resource that they need is one of the best ways to build your business relationships. And minimizing the number of decisions they have to make can save them a lot of time and mental energy.

Your lawyer's brain may be telling you that giving multiple referrals is a way to stay top of mind with multiple service providers. But think about that. Are you happier when someone tells a prospect to call you or when someone includes your name on a list of lawyers to interview?

The next time you give a referral, consider giving only one name. You'll be doing everyone—including yourself—a favor. And you can always tell the person who you give the referral to that they should come back to you if they need a different referral.

CHAPTER 18

If You Are Not Memorable, Don't Expect to Be Remembered

> "In a crowded marketplace, fitting in is failing. In a busy marketplace, not standing out is the same as being invisible."
>
> —*Seth Godin*

I don't collect artwork. Aside from the expense, I like things I can easily share with other people... like memes.

Since I joined the ProVisors business network in 2019, I've been collecting—and sharing—taglines. A good tagline is a great way to quickly differentiate yourself and make yourself memorable.

Here are a few examples that have resonated with me the last several years:

- *Taking Aspiring Americans from Visa Application to Pledge of Allegiance*—Saja Raoof, an immigration lawyer
- *I Bring Death and Taxes to Life*—Jennifer Taddeo, a trusts and estates lawyer
- *The Reconstructionist (Helping People Get Out from Under Debilitating Debt)*—Theda Page, a bankruptcy attorney
- *You Go to Court to Make a Point. You Go to Mediation to Make a Deal.*—Michael Bunim, a mediator
- *Hurt? Can't Work? Call Me*—Tanusha Thuraisingam, a Social Security Disability Insurance (SSDI) attorney
- *If It Is Healthcare, I Care*—Edward (E.J.) Cyran, a healthcare lawyer

- *Do You Want a Patent That Hangs Up on the Wall or a Patent That Stands Up in Court?*—Steven Evans, a patent litigator

While not everyone's practice lends itself to a good tagline, and while having a good tagline is not essential to your marketing success, it can increase the likelihood that you will stay top of mind.

And staying top of mind is the name of the game in marketing your law practice.

GIVEN THE NATURE OF LEGAL SERVICES, BEING MEMORABLE OVER TIME IS ESSENTIAL

One of the great pieces of wisdom that I have gotten from ProVisors is the importance of choosing your lane. There are many trusted advisors in ProVisors (lawyers and otherwise) who provide similar services. It is, therefore, very important to define yourself in a way that differentiates you from the competition.

At the same time, you want to be remembered when an opportunity arises.

While people may see their dentist twice a year for a cleaning, they may reach out for legal advice only once every few years (for example, when buying a house, drafting a will, seeking recovery for an injury caused by negligence, etc.).

Similarly, a business may need a lawyer only when seeking bank financing, negotiating a lease, drafting an employee handbook, or negotiating a consulting agreement. And it may be hard to know when that need will arise.

Therefore, you want to be memorable over time. If you keep your message simple, make it unforgettable, and reinforce it through marketing (speaking, writing, social media, involvement in bar associations and other organizations, etc.) and business development (i.e., relationship building), you will greatly increase the chances that a potential client or referral source will think of you when the opportunity comes along.

In your marketing, think long and hard about how you want to be known. Perhaps you are a litigator who handles commercial disputes, real estate disputes, personal injury, and a host of other things that may come in the door.

But if you don't choose your lane, will you really be remembered? You don't have to limit yourself to one type of work for one kind of client. But if you list five types of work for six types of clients (because you don't want to miss out on anything), paradoxically, you will muddle your message.

Less is more in marketing. You can't be known for everything. Come up with a message that clearly defines your lane at networking functions, in one-on-one conversations, or when you produce content about your practice area. You can always take a case that falls outside your lane. But focusing your message is how you will stand out from the pack.

OTHER WAYS TO DIFFERENTIATE YOURSELF AND BE MEMORABLE

Taglines are often based on a niche, and sometimes they can set you apart. If I encounter someone who is injured and might qualify for SSDI benefits, I immediately think of Tanusha Thuraisingam (see tagline above).

I have a client who serves as an outside general counsel to the restaurant industry. Her clients are award-winning chefs and restauranteurs who are trying to add locations.

But intangible qualities can also make you memorable. Perhaps you have a good sense of humor. Maybe you are a real connector (that would be me—I love connecting people in my network, and I like to think of myself as a coach who uses humor to make a point, although not everyone appreciates my stupid dad jokes).

I know an accountant, Dave McLaren, who always shows up in a bowtie. I know a patent lawyer, Tony Laurentano, who calls his networking group "Fun Club." He held a ProVisors meeting with a "summer fun" theme, and attendees showed up in beach attire.

The differentiator might also be a personal interest of yours. Do you do stand-up comedy? Play in a cover band? Volunteer for a dog rescue organization? Collect wine? Hold a leadership role in your church or synagogue? Like to host social gatherings? Do you like old cars? Baseball?

I have a client who makes body scrubs and liqueurs. She has parties where she gives them out, and she also sends them as holiday gifts.

The differentiator might also be your style as a lawyer.

Are you a collaborator? A tough negotiator? A take-no-prisoners litigator? Do you have a good sense of humor?

Deb Danger, a lawyer who does trusts and estates work, likes to put her clients at ease. Many people are uncomfortable with the topics of death and dying, so Deb tells her clients that she will give them a 10 percent discount if they make her laugh. Not only does that make her memorable, but it also makes clients feel a lot more comfortable with the subject matter of their conversation.

I have a client who likes to mail goofy postcards to his network when he is traveling.

Do you have a background or training that separates you from other lawyers? A military background? A family that was in the restaurant business when you were growing up (the client I mentioned above who represents restaurants grew up waiting tables, her father was a chef, and her husband operates a high-end take-out restaurant)?

Maybe you had a prior career as a software engineer, as a social worker, as a CPA, or you owned your own business after college.

Do you have a strong "why?"

I know a lawyer who enjoys probate litigation because there was a lot of conflict in her family over an estate when she was in high school.

I'm an attorney coach who enjoys working with lawyers because I'm a lawyer myself, and I think like a lawyer (and through coaching and therapy, I've learned to shut off that part of my personality in order to grow my business).

If you can effectively communicate why you do what you do, that will make you more memorable.

TELL STORIES

Our brains are hardwired for stories. From the dawn of human evolution, storytelling has been a fundamental means of communication and connection. Early humans used stories not just for entertainment, but to share critical information, to preserve cultural values, and to forge social bonds. These narratives were integral to survival, helping communities learn from experiences, teach important lessons, and build cohesive groups.

In the modern context, stories continue to play a crucial role in marketing. Stories make presentations more memorable and help people remember you when an appropriate opportunity to refer work to you arises. Crafting stories that illustrate the problems you solve is one of the best ways to make yourself memorable and to differentiate your services.

When telling stories, focus on the elements that will resonate with your audience. Avoid getting bogged down in excessive specifics. Instead, highlight the aspects of your story that clearly convey the value you provided to your clients. This approach ensures that your narrative is not only engaging but also relevant and impactful.

Creating compelling stories requires thoughtful preparation. One effective strategy is to maintain a running list of your matters and continuously update it with new experiences. For litigators, this could mean keeping a litigation summary that outlines key cases and outcomes. For transactional lawyers, a detailed deal sheet can be invaluable.

These summaries are not only useful for storytelling but also play a significant role when pursuing new job opportunities or responding to RFPs. They allow you to quickly recall and present relevant experiences, showcasing your expertise and track record in a way that is both organized and persuasive.

In essence, storytelling is an art and a science. It draws on deep-seated human traditions and leverages your own experiences to create a narrative that is engaging, memorable, and effective in communicating your value. By mastering the art of storytelling, you can connect more deeply with your audience and enhance your professional impact.

If you say to yourself, "I'm not a good storyteller," think again. We all have stories to tell. Taking the time to craft your stories before you are out networking will ensure that you have lots of things to talk about. Resisting your lawyerly urge to be thorough will also help.

AUTHENTICITY AND CONSISTENCY ARE KEY

There are many ways to make yourself memorable. Differentiating yourself from other lawyers who do what you do is a good starting point. In doing so, don't forget to be authentic. We've been discussing that throughout this book. Choose a niche that you enjoy. Pursue personal interests you like. If you are the kind of person who sends birthday cards, pays condolence calls, or likes to share cartoons, do that. In terms of style, just be you! Everyone else is taken.

And don't forget to keep it up over time. It may be 15 minutes or 15 years before someone may need your services or hear of someone who needs your services.

Even the most memorable lawyer will be forgotten if she doesn't keep showing up. Stay the course.

STAYING TOP OF MIND WITH FORMER CLIENTS

"I was stunned by the response."

That is what my client told me after sending out 20 email messages to former clients.

This lawyer was reluctant to reach out to these clients because it had been a long time since she last communicated with them. And she assumed that few would respond.

Her inner dialogue went something like this:

- *Why would they want to hear from me?*
- *They are going to think that I'm just reaching out because I want their business.*
- *I don't like it when people think of me as a pushy salesperson.*
- *I don't want to feel rejected if they don't respond.*

In fact, the majority of her clients did respond… and they responded quickly. Not only were they happy to hear from her, but they all said they would be happy to meet her over coffee or Zoom.

While it is of course better to keep in touch and find ways to stay top of mind over a long period of time, in all likelihood, former clients will be happy to reconnect if you reach out, even if it has been a long time since you last checked in.

If you had a good relationship with your old clients, and especially if you got a good result for them and provided great service, don't be surprised when they welcome your outreach.

While we don't like setting ourselves up for rejection as lawyers, in reality, reaching out to old clients is NOT setting yourself up for rejection—if you do it in the right way. If you focus on finding ways to be helpful (which may very well extend beyond providing legal services to them), you can rebuild old relationships in a way that can be mutually beneficial.

This is hard for lawyers. But it is well worth trying this strategy. It is hard to build relationships from scratch. Starting where there is a history is a great way to strengthen your network.

STAYING IN TOUCH IS OFTEN NOT A PRIORITY, BUT YOU'RE MISSING OPPORTUNITIES

Former clients can be a good source of additional business and referrals. But if you are like many lawyers who I coach, once a client matter has been resolved, your energy generally shifts to the next client or the next matter. Staying in touch falls way down on your priority list.

In my opinion, failing to stay in contact with former clients is a big, missed opportunity. It takes a lot of time and energy to build a trusted relationship with clients. That trust is essential in getting clients to hire you in the first place. Once that trust is built, clients are likely to think of you if they have a legal need or if they hear of someone else who has a legal need.

Clients who know, like, and trust you are generally your best referral sources. If they were happy with your service, most clients are happy to make a referral.

The reality is that the opportunity to hire you again or make a referral is episodic. That is the nature of most legal work. It could be months or years before a client needs your services again or is in the position to make a referral. In the interim, the memory of the great work you did may fade.

Therefore, staying top of mind over time needs to be a critical part of your marketing plan. Knowing when and how often to follow up is an important part of that.

WHY DO MOST OF US DROP THE BALL?

If you are wired like many of the lawyers I coach, reaching out to former clients feels "salesy." Many of us don't like it when stockbrokers and other service providers reach out to us to set up a time to talk. It feels as if they are just trying to sell us something.

If your mindset is that you are reaching out only because you want more work from this client, then that makes sense. Your internal dialogue is going to be, "Client X is going to think I'm just trying to get more work from her."

On the other hand, if you think about connecting as an effort to build the relationship in a mutual way, then it is easier to send an email to schedule a time to reconnect.

Another reason that many of us avoid reaching out is that we are not sure what to say once we are meeting clients for coffee, by phone, or on Zoom.

So here is the reframe: Reconnecting with a former client in a way that strengthens your professional relationship may open doors to new opportunities, but it is also a way to add value to the relationship beyond doing more client work. Doing so requires a thoughtful and tactful approach.

What follows are some suggestions about how to structure your follow-up conversations with former clients. By planning these follow-up conversations in advance, you can come to meetings feeling more comfortable and knowing that you will be able to give more value.

APPROACH OLD CLIENTS AS YOU WOULD OLD FRIENDS

There is a good chance that former clients will be happy to reconnect. If you achieved a good outcome for them and provided good customer service, most clients are happy to speak. I generally recommend sending an email that goes something like this:

> *Hi, Jim. It has been a long time since we last connected. My apologies for being out of touch. I enjoyed working with you on [very briefly describe matter], and I'm curious about how things turned out with [describe]. I'd love to hear what you are up to and what challenges you are facing. I'm also trying to expand my business, and if you are open to it, I'd like to pick your brain about that. Are you free the third week of [fill in the blank] for coffee or a Zoom? I look forward to catching up!*

This is merely suggested language and obviously needs to be put in your own voice. The key points to make are:

- Apologize for being out of touch. This creates more of an opening to reconnect. It was very successful for my client.
- Establish rapport by referring back to your last interaction (generally the matter you worked on).
- Tell them you are curious about what they are up to.
- Be transparent that you want their help (i.e., not necessarily more business from them).

How persistent should you be? That, of course, depends on the nature of the prior relationship. But go back to chapter 15 for more on that.

Once you have your meetings set up, it's time to prepare. Do your homework and think about the questions you might ask. Below are my suggestions, but there may be very specific questions that you can come up with based on your prior relationship, what you know about the person, and what you've read about this person's company or industry.

General Reconnection and Updates

- "How have you been?" In many ways, this is the most important part of the conversation. Ask about their family or anything personal you know about them or their personal interests: "Are you playing guitar?" "Have you been to any [name of sports team] games lately?" "How was your son's graduation?" "How is your mom adjusting since your dad passed away?" Ask if they have any vacation plans, if they did anything fun last weekend, or if they will be doing anything fun this weekend. Make sure to open the conversation in this way. But don't forget to shift the conversation after a few minutes. If you have been keeping notes about the client in your contact manager, review your notes before you meet.

- "What's new with [their company] since we last worked together?" Follow up with more specific questions based on your preparation for the meeting: "How did things work out with [client matter]?" "I saw that [thing you read about the company in the news or company website, then ask a follow-up question about that thing]."

Offering Value

- "What are some of your greatest challenges right now?" Depending on how they answer, ask lots of follow-up questions, and be a great listener. Listen for ways you can be helpful. This includes referring them to resources or other contacts that might be helpful to them. These can be resources that are helpful to them professionally or personally (e.g., maybe you know a good plumber they can call, or maybe you can recommend a good restaurant or podcast).
- "What is a good introduction for you?" This question is focused on helping them meet individuals who can help grow their business. The introduction might be someone who works for a particular business, a particular industry, or another professional who serves the same clients.
- "Are there any resources I can connect you with?" Here, you may want to be a little more specific based on what you've already heard. If you are being a good listener, you may find out that they are looking for another business resource or even a personal resource where you can be of help (this could be anything from an accountant to a house painter to an article on choosing a summer camp for their kids).
- "A lot has been happening in [area of law where you counseled them previously]. Would you be interested in an article we published on that or in setting up a time to give you a quick briefing?"

Exploring Further Collaboration

- "We worked with you on [matter you worked on]. We would love to expand our relationship with [company]. Can I tell you about some of our firm's other capabilities?"
- "Is there a project or initiative you're excited about? How are you planning to tackle it?" This can open the door for the client either to make referrals or to identify more potential work for you.

Seeking Referrals and Expanding Your Network

- "I really enjoy working with clients like you who are [describe qualities such as "innovative," "forward-thinking," etc., or describe their industry]. Do you know other professionals in your industry who might be facing similar issues or who could use someone to bounce ideas off?" Try to be somewhat specific about what a good introduction looks like for you. It doesn't have to be an actual referral. Introductions can be very valuable.
- "I'm trying to better understand the broader trends affecting your industry. Could you recommend events or groups that you find valuable for networking or professional development?"

Ending on a Positive Note

- "Thank you for taking the time to meet today. I look forward to staying in touch, and I am always here if you need anything. How can I best support you going forward?" This reinforces your willingness to be a resource, regardless of immediate business

Follow-Up and Summary

After the meeting, send a thank-you note summarizing key points of interest and any commitments you made. This keeps the lines of communication open and ensures that your client feels valued and remembered.

Mark in your calendar a time to follow up in the future (if nothing has happened organically before that date). You can also bcc yourself on the email, set a reminder flag for some date in the future, and file the email.

BE AUTHENTIC

It is important to have conversations in a way that feels authentic to you and not forced. The language suggested above is just a suggestion. You might feel more comfortable phrasing things a different way.

ChatGPT is something worth playing with if you are having trouble coming up with language that feels like you.

While you may have to practice some of the questions you plan to ask, and preparation is of course important, fundamentally, you want to come across as genuine. This includes showing genuine interest in the other person. Be a great listener.

By focusing on building a relationship that's based on mutual respect and interest rather than just business transactions, you position yourself as a trusted advisor and a valuable network contact. That will keep you top of mind with other professionals. Ultimately, it will help you grow your business.

SAMPLE QUESTIONS TO ASK AT A NETWORKING MEETING

General Reconnection and Updates

- ✓ "How have you been?"
- ✓ "Are you [playing guitar, skiing this winter, etc.]?"
- ✓ "Have you been to any [name of sports team] games lately?"
- ✓ "How was your son's graduation?"
- ✓ "How is your mom adjusting since your dad passed away?"
- ✓ "Do you have any vacation plans?"
- ✓ "Will you be doing anything fun this weekend?"
- ✓ "What's new with [their company] since we last worked together?"
- ✓ "How did things work out with [client matter]?"

Offering Value

- ✓ "What are some of your greatest challenges right now?"
- ✓ "What is a good introduction for you?"
- ✓ "Are there any resources I can connect you with?"
- ✓ "A lot has been happening in [area of law where you counseled them previously]. Would you be interested in an article we published on that or getting a quick briefing?"

(continued)

Exploring Further Collaboration
✓ "We worked with you on [matter you worked on]. We would love to expand our relationship with [company]. Can I tell you about some of our firm's other capabilities?"
✓ "Is there a project or initiative you're excited about? How are you planning to tackle it?"
Seeking Referrals and Expanding Network
✓ "I really enjoy working with clients like you. Do you know other professionals in your industry who might be facing similar issues or could use someone to bounce ideas off?"
✓ "I'm trying to better understand the broader trends affecting your industry. Could you recommend events or groups that you find valuable for networking or professional development?"

WAYS TO STAY TOP OF MIND WITH YOUR NETWORK

Schedule a catch up via Zoom	Invite them to coffee or lunch
Comment on and like their LinkedIn posts	Help them or their family member with a job search
Refer business to them or find out who is a good introduction for them	Make a professional or personal referral (e.g., accountant, tech consultant, plumber, lawyer)
Introduce them to a potential referral partner	Participate in a charitable cause they like
Email them an article or other helpful resources	Email something related to their personal interests
Invite comments on an article you are writing	Invite them to a sporting event
Celebrate client victories or tell them about your other victories	Send holiday gifts
Invite them to a reception at your firm or elsewhere	Ask about their spouse and children

(continued)

Invite them to participate on a panel or a podcast	Teach them something non-legal (e.g., how to use an app you like or how to roast your own coffee)
Send notes of congratulations—professional	Send notes of congratulations—personal
Send condolence cards/attend funerals	Recommend a good movie, book, streaming TV series, podcast, etc.
Introduce them to a hobby or nonprofit cause	Mention their name as a source to a reporter
Follow up on a referral you gave them and find out how it went	Thank them for a referral they gave you and send a gift certificate (and reach out again to update them)
Let them know about your significant life events or awards you have won	Invite them to your concert, exhibit, or social event
Ask about a sick family member or pet	Come to their functions
Attend a presentation they give	Join organizations where they are active
Send firm-branded items (swag)	Interview them for an article
Buy their stuff	Send them something humorous
Send birthday and/or holiday greetings	Give a brief tutorial on a legal subject or send them a related article
Send a handwritten note	Ask about their dog or go on a walk

CHAPTER 19

Investment Hours, Time Management, Testimonials, and Focus

Since graduating from law school in the late 1980s, I have been hearing talk about doing away with the billable hour. In the early 1990s, I organized several seminars entitled "Beyond the Billable Hour" in which a panel of consultants and lawyers discussed the hourly billing model and how law firms might want to adapt.

Since that time, the billable hour has persisted. While there continues to be efforts to move away from time billing, it seems like the billable hour isn't going away anytime soon.

There are certain practice areas that do lend themselves to a fixed-fee model, and attorneys at smaller firms have been using these fixed-fee billing for a long time. Charging a flat rate for a will or a real estate closing is common practice. For a large segment of the bar, however, lawyers bill for their time. AI may finally disrupt that, but for now, the billable hour dominates.

When it comes to marketing, there are some significant problems with the billable hour model. The billable hour draws attention to short-term rewards rather than the long-term benefits of investing in relationship and reputation building activities. While your marketing efforts will produce results if you are consistent over time, in the short run, there is generally no monetary benefit for doing anything other than billable work.

If you are an associate who has a billable hour target, you have a strong incentive to focus most of your energy on billing your time. This is only exacerbated by the fact that at many firms, bonuses are determined in part by meeting a billable hour target.

At the same time, if you focus only on the short term, your prospect of growing your practice in the long term will be adversely affected.

One way to carve out time for marketing is to shift your mindset when thinking about time. Paul Morton, who worked in law firm administration for several decades in the Boston area, suggests that the term *non-billable hours* is a misnomer. He instead recommends that the time spent on marketing, professional development, firm administration, and management be labeled *investment hours*. He contends that using the term non-billable hours suggests that these hours have no value.

With that in mind, how much of your time should you carve out for investing in yourself and in your firm? That of course depends on how busy you are with fee-generating work. But as we've discussed in earlier chapters, a steady and consistent approach is much more effective than saving marketing for a rainy day. Making a few phone calls and sending out a few emails, even when you have a lot of work on your plate, is important. In other words, you do not have to be all in at all times to have impact on your marketing results. Even small acts of connection can serve as an important way for you to stay top of mind with your network.

Put another way, don't let great be the enemy of the good. Like getting in shape, marketing results are cumulative. Just because you don't have time to run a marathon, that doesn't mean you won't benefit from taking short walks.

This requires us to change our mindset. Most of us were trained to be very thorough in representing our clients. Attention to detail is usually a sign of good lawyering. But when it comes to marketing, we don't have to be thorough in everything we do. If you don't have time to send three emails, send two. If you don't have time to write an article, do a short LinkedIn post.

In chapter 4, I recommended that you practice *mindlessness*. Get yourself on autopilot. Develop good marketing habits that you can keep up with even when you are busy with billable work.

BE REALISTIC ABOUT YOUR COMMITMENT TO MARKETING

Sometimes, other commitments do actually conflict with marketing. If you have small children, sick family members, or other personal commitments, marketing *will* have to wait. If you are staying up until two in the morning preparing for trial, spending time on anything else may not be realistic.

That is not necessarily a bad thing. The best way to be effective in your relationship building is to be present in all senses of the word. Taking care of yourself and others will ensure that when you do have time to show up, you will do it with a positive attitude and in a way that is likely to foster connection. If you are in the midst of trial or involved in some other "all hands on deck" matter, you may need to hit the pause button on your marketing, and that is okay. But even in those circumstances, see if there is just one thing you can do each day to keep up your momentum.

DO, DEFER, DELEGATE, OR DROP

Your time is limited. Learning good time-management techniques is a great way to get to your important marketing tasks. One important way to manage your time is to think critically about how you are spending your time. If you have made the effort to think in advance about what is truly time sensitive, you will know where to focus your investment hours.

The four Ds provide some guidance on this: Do, Defer, Delegate, or Drop. The idea of the four Ds is to triage every task that confronts you. Dealing with email is one of the best uses of this technique.[1] There are some email messages that are worth responding to immediately when they land in your inbox. Some can truly be handled quickly. Sometimes, messages are truly time sensitive. This is when it is time to "Do."

But not every email we receive requires immediate attention. Some messages are not time sensitive, and some are not important. If a message is important but not time sensitive, remove those messages from your inbox and file them in a different folder so that they are not constantly staring you in the face. Put a calendar flag on them to remind you to get back to the task. There are a lot of messages that you can "Defer."

As lawyers, this can be challenging. As I've mentioned several times, we are a group with a high sense of urgency. Setting aside our sense of urgency can challenge our self-identity (*I'm someone who knows how to get things done*). But a failure to

---

[1] There is a lot more to say about time management that is beyond the scope of this book. Suffice it to say, email has been a mixed blessing in the workplace. It provides an efficient and quick method of communication that documents what has been said. But it also provides a huge source of distraction and can be a big-time disrupter.

defer some things (whether they involve billable work or marketing) will mean that the things that are truly important will not get done in a timely manner.

Looking for things to "Delegate" is another area for improvement for many of us. I have a lot of clients who believe it will take more time to explain a task than it will to do the task. They believe that they can probably do it better themselves. Sometimes that is true. Often, the reality is that it will take more effort the first time, but the next time, delegation will be much more efficient.

As lawyers, we have trouble with delegation because we self-identify as doers. We think we are smart and can figure things out. It can seem risky to delegate a task to someone if it won't be done as well by them.

While we are indeed smart and generally more experienced than our subordinates, that doesn't mean that we should be doing everything ourselves. For example, failing to delegate writing the first draft of an article for a trade journal may mean we have less time for higher level activities that we cannot delegate.

Similarly, just because we are good writers, that doesn't mean we know how to write copy for a website or other marketing collateral. Delegating to an internal or external marketing professional may be a way to get a much better work product.

Sometimes, delegating billable work to a paralegal or associate is the best use of our time. We can review what they have drafted after the fact. That frees up time for us to meet important clients and referral sources for coffee or take them to a sporting event, something that only we can do.

Finally, setting boundaries on our time is a critical part of being an effective professional and being successful in marketing your business. Stop saying yes to every opportunity to write, speak, volunteer, or meet for coffee. Figure out which activities support your overall marketing goals and "Drop" the rest. Don't let other people set the agenda for you.

ASKING HAPPY CLIENTS FOR INTRODUCTIONS, REVIEWS, AND TESTIMONIALS

Law is a relationship business. Once you have built a trusted relationship with a client, potential client, or referral source, those individuals are more likely to think of you when they have a need or hear of someone who has a need. Building new relationships can always be part of your marketing strategy; but it is important to leverage the relationships you already have already built. And as we discussed in chapter16, it is important to focus on cultivating relationships with C.H.I.L.L. referral partners who can make introductions in addition to referrals.

Another way to leverage these relationships is to ask for testimonials. These can be LinkedIn recommendations, Google reviews, or if your firm and jurisdiction permit it, testimonials on your website. Getting permission from clients to include their name in case studies on your website can also be a good way to leverage your client relationships. The time to ask is when the client is happy with a result you achieved or work you have done. These testimonials and stories provide important validation to any prospective client who is thinking of hiring you. Social proof can reinforce a buying decision.

Many lawyers, however, do not ask clients to provide these. For starters, most of us do not want to appear too salesy. We do not like the possibility of a client rejecting the request and therefore creating some awkwardness in the relationship.

The truth is that most clients are very happy to give referrals, make introductions, and provide reviews and testimonials. If you have any doubt about that, think about how happy you would be if a service provider you liked asked you for a review.

As the world of professional services marketing continues to move online, the importance of having these testimonial will only grow. This will actually be helpful to the many attorneys who are more introverted and less comfortable with networking (although that is not an excuse to avoid networking and in-person relationship building).

FOCUS IS IMPORTANT BUT OVER TIME, YOUR MARKETING MESSAGE NEEDS TO EVOLVE

I had lunch a few months ago with a partner of a small law firm. I have always considered this individual to be a bankruptcy lawyer; but as we got caught up, he described himself as someone who does real estate and corporate finance. I then discovered that back in the 1990s, he used to describe himself as a commercial litigator.

Was he lacking in focus? Was his marketing message weak?

Many of the clients that I coach have difficulty in choosing a marketing focus. The common fear that I encounter is the fear of missing opportunities. The mistaken belief is that if you don't list everything you do, you may miss the chance to serve someone who has a problem that you can solve. It feels risky to leave out the laundry list of our areas of expertise.

But there is an old adage in marketing: less is more.

While it is true that less is more, this does not mean that your marketing message must remain fixed over time. As the economy shifts and as the law evolves, lawyers need to be able to shift as well. What may be a hot specialty today may no longer be needed tomorrow. This will be true throughout your career, and it is particularly true right now as AI plays an increasing role in our economy and in the practice of law.

In the past decade, I have seen several new areas of expertise emerge. The cannabis industry has spawned a lot of business and legal activity. Data privacy has become a critical issue that every business must now address. If you see an opportunity to develop a new area of specialization, don't shy away. But understand that it will still be important to present your expertise in a focused way that is memorable. See chapter 18 for more on being memorable.

Coupled with the need to be nimble over time is the need to recognize that finding the right way to describe your services may involve some trial and error. In other words, in order to maximize your marketing effectiveness, you may need to test market a few phrases before you settle on one that works.

Political strategists and marketing consultants understand this. The words you choose to describe what you do can have a great impact on how you are perceived and whether you will be remembered. (For example, why do you think that Republicans began to refer to the estate tax as the "death tax"?) They test market messages to see what resonates with voters or consumers.

The goal, of course, is to deliver a focused message about what you do (i.e., one that makes you memorable and differentiates you from other lawyers). When you find a message that works, stick with it. Repetition is essential in marketing. But be aware of the need to evolve as the law and the marketplace for legal services evolve. Otherwise, you may find yourself trying to sell buggy whips to consumers who want hybrid cars.

RECYCLING CAN IMPROVE YOUR MARKETING EFFICIENCY

For many of us, carving out time for marketing activities is challenging. When there is billable work to do, spending time on things that don't immediately generate revenue is hard to prioritize.

One hack that can help you generate more marketing activity without adding a lot of time to your day is to recycle. If you have some content that you can use in a variety of ways, that enables you to better leverage your time.

Being original is overrated! This is a hard concept for lawyers who pride themselves on displaying thought leadership. Thought leadership and providing timely information about developments in the law can be very beneficial to your brand. But that needs to be weighed against the simple fact that staying top of mind does not require you to consistently write or speak about cutting-edge topics.

For example, if many clients are asking questions about a particular subject, you can turn that into a blog post. That blog post can become a LinkedIn post. Similarly you can then turn that into a presentation and maybe include links in a newsletter to a workshop you are planning.

Another marketing hack is to take evergreen marketing content and promote it more than once. If you post on LinkedIn, different people in your network will see it and are online at different times. Posting the same contact more than once is a way to reach a wider audience. It can also reinforce your message (don't worry; no one is really paying that close attention).

Advertisers know this. Why do we keep seeing the same advertisement for a particular product? It takes time for a message to sink in, and the point when a client, prospective client, or referral source might have a need for your services comes up only periodically.

In addition, because of the way our brains are wired, we are more likely to trust information that is familiar. Therefore, keeping your message in front of this audience over time, even if it is the same message, can be very efficient and also very effective.

In my recycling queue, I also have podcasts to add to the mix. If I interview somebody, I can do a blog post, a LinkedIn post which links to the blog, and then I send it out with my newsletter. Maybe I'll do a presentation about the same topic.

The American Bar Association does this really well. It generates a lot of content that goes out in magazine form and then gets reused in newsletters.

I was therefore bemused when I saw an email newsletter in my inbox. "How to Blow Your Own Horn" sounded like an article that would be of great interest to me. Since I was writing this book, I immediately clicked on the link.

As it turns out, I actually wrote the article. . . . But the ABA repurposed the content with a new name (the original title was "Nine Ways to Market Yourself without Feeling Like a Salesperson").

With a little creative license, you can get your message out in slightly different ways. You can increase your marketing efficiency and still have impact.

Recycling Your Thought Leadership

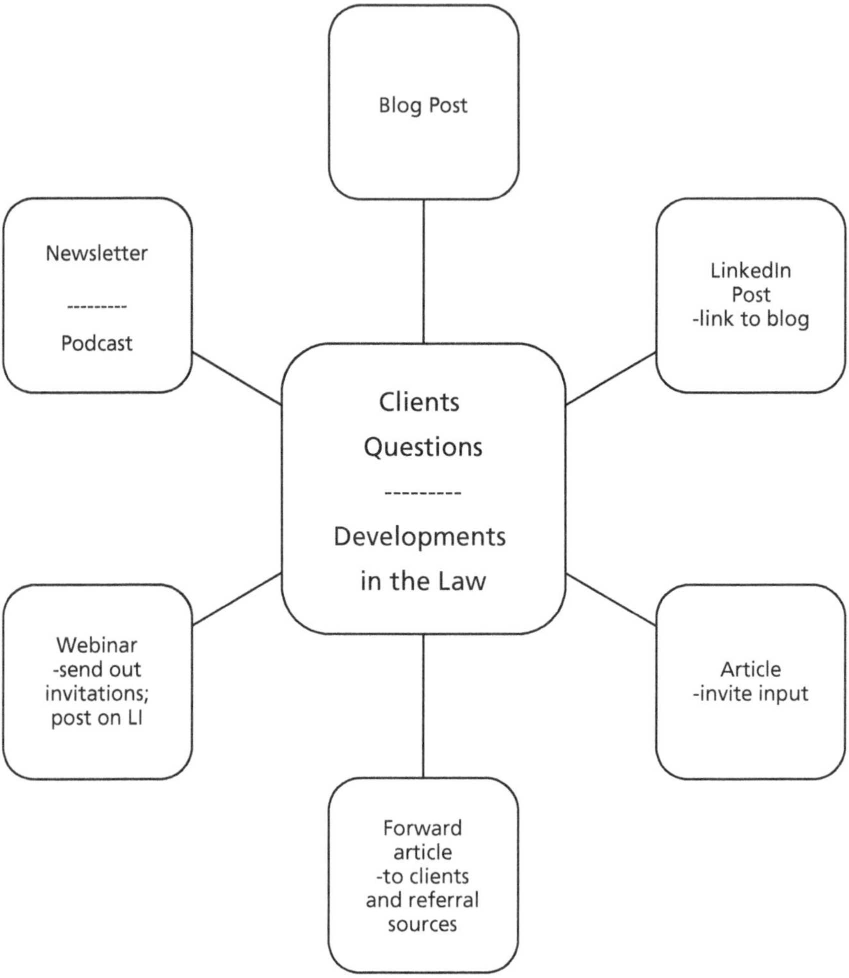

CHAPTER 20

LinkedIn, Podcasting, and AI

Like most people who share content on LinkedIn, whenever I post something, I start to focus on how many views the post has had. It is a fun way to see if my messaging is having any impact, and in a small way, it is a measurement of whether my marketing is working. I do the same when I send out newsletters.

Anyone who posts on Facebook or Instagram knows the feeling. You get a little rush of dopamine when you see the "likes" adding up. But focusing on the quantity of views on LinkedIn may not be a very good measure of how much impact you are having with your target audience.

Several years ago, I was speaking with my friend Micah Sifry. I told Micah that I was excited that some of my recent posts had over 4,000 views on LinkedIn. In addition, for the first time ever, one of my posts was "trending."

Micah knocked me down to earth and offered some great insights about this. In a nutshell, Micah emphasizes the importance of *the quality of engagement* you get on LinkedIn and other social media, *not the quantity*. He told me to look at how many comments I had, how many likes I had, and how many of those likes and comments were from repeaters (i.e., people who have "liked" or commented on my other posts). He also told me to be responsive to those individuals (i.e., look for ways to continue the conversation with them either on LinkedIn or, better yet, in real life). He told me that rather than looking at "vanity metrics," I should look for engagement.

Of course, using hashtags and tagging people in your network can help a lot. So can attaching yourself to existing networks. I'm sure my many posts about the

ProVisors business networking group get a lot of views, likes, and comments, because I tag people who encouraged me to join, and I use several hashtags. In addition, ProVisors is a very strong network.

Micah also pointed out that joining other people's conversations and being generous in pointing to other good content is a great way to engage.

Micah is a thought leader who writes about the ways that technology is changing politics, government, and civil society. He was one of the first people I knew who understood the web, social media, blogging, and electronic communication. While he focuses on the political and civic realm, his comments are very relevant to lawyers and other professionals who are trying to get visibility through social media, blogging, and newsletters. If you are a lawyer who serves businesses or other institutional clients, you don't need to get the attention of a lot of people. You just need to get the attention of the "right" people.

Posting regularly on LinkedIn is a simple way to remind your clients, prospective clients, and referral sources that you exist. But if you are going to use LinkedIn or other social media as part of your marketing efforts, focus on really connecting with people. The number of "views" may make you feel good. But if you want to keep the lights on, try connecting in person.

RECYCLING CONTENT ON LINKEDIN

This is only a partial list of the many things you can repurpose on LinkedIn. ChatGPT can help you generate more ideas.

- **Client Success Stories**: Highlight the successes you've achieved for your clients or that your clients have achieved on their own.
- **Industry Tips**: Offer valuable insights and advice to establish your expertise.
- **Legal Updates**: Inform your audience about new statutes, regulations, or case law and their implications.
- **Events**: Share experiences and insights from professional events and conferences. Post photographs from the event.
- **Presentations**: Showcase your participation in speaking engagements to enhance your professional image. Do a post before the presentation and one afterwards. Include a photograph of the panel.
- **Achievements**: Celebrate and share your awards and the recognition you have received thanks to your clients, your colleagues, and the people who have helped you.

- **Curated Articles**: Share useful articles from reputable sources and offer some commentary.
- **Articles and Blog Posts**: Share articles that you or your colleagues have written to highlight your thought leadership and your firm's thought leadership. Discuss emerging trends in your practice area, in the legal industry, or in your clients' industries.
- **Partnerships**: Highlight collaborations with other firms or professionals to demonstrate your network and influence.
- **Career Milestones**: Share significant career milestones to humanize your professional journey.
- **Continuing Education**: Highlight certifications, courses, or degrees you've earned to show your commitment to professional growth.
- **Community Involvement**: Share your pro bono work or community service activities to show social responsibility.
- **Personal Reflections**: Occasionally share personal stories that are related to your professional life in order to build authenticity.
- **Firm Culture**: Share glimpses of your firm's culture, including team activities, to attract potential clients and employees.
- **Interactive Sessions**: Conduct Q&A sessions on LinkedIn Live or through posts to engage your audience. Invite clients, colleagues, or referral partners to participate.
- **Resource Recommendations**: Provide lists of helpful resources, such as legal guides or toolkits, books you've read, or podcasts you've heard.
- **Client Feedback**: Share testimonials from clients. These types of posts should be infrequent as they are more self-promotional.

HOW PODCASTING CAN HELP YOUR LAW PRACTICE (IT'S NOT WHAT YOU THINK)

In July of 2024, my podcast hit a new milestone. *Counsel to Counsel* has now been downloaded over 36,000 times (if you are counting "bot downloads"—but over 23,000 downloads if you just count the humans). While I am proud of this number and I know that podcasting has been helpful in building my brand, it is important to keep this in perspective. Podcasting is not a big lead generation tool for me, at least not directly. In addition, that number is a drop in the bucket when compared with much more successful podcasts, social media influencers, and the content put out by major networks.

But there are many reasons why I plan to continue producing new episodes for a long time to come and many reasons why I believe that podcasting can be a worthwhile endeavor for many lawyers.

Understand Your Target Audience

While it is hard to determine how many podcasts are in existence, a few Google results suggest that the number is well over 4 million with well over 70 million episodes. Clearly, there is a lot of competition for our attention, and starting a podcast doesn't guarantee that anyone is listening. But if you are looking for a way to create content that targets a micro audience and you enjoy interviewing people, keep reading.

The barriers to starting a podcast are very low. With a decent laptop, a very inexpensive subscription to a podcasting host (I use Libsyn), and less than $400 worth of equipment (a good microphone, headphones, microphone stand, and mixer), you can be in business in a day. There are free tools for recording (I use the paid version of Zoom which is currently less than $20 a month) and free tools for mixing and editing your recordings (I use Audacity).

The largest cost of podcasting is really your own time. So, if your law practice is busy enough, you might want to outsource the production and focus on the practice of law. For the time being, I'm happy to do my own production, in part because it forces me to listen to the interviews again.

Four Reasons Why I Continue to Produce Counsel to Counsel

There are four reasons I love having my own podcast. I'm listing them in order of importance.

1. I Love to Interview People

For me, the greatest value of having a podcast is that I get to interview people who know more about a subject than I do. In more than 145 episodes, I've spoken with guests about social media, legal marketing, time management, going in-house, career success strategies in a law firm, leadership, executive coaching, selling legal services, alternative legal careers, attorney well-being, mindfulness, retirement, financial planning, lateral moves, going solo, building your network, and interviewing skills.

Each one of these interviews has given me a chance to deepen my understanding of a subject. I like to refer to *Counsel to Counsel* as Steve Seckler University.

I always choose topics that interest me, and I always choose guests who are willing to teach me something new.

I've always loved learning in this way. From the earliest age, I can remember asking my parents a lot of questions. Back in those days, sometimes the answer was "go look it up in the encyclopedia." But as the son of academics, a desire to learn has always been deeply embedded in my DNA, so I was never short on things I wanted to learn.

If you host your own podcast, you have the chance to learn something new from your clients, your referral sources, and other professionals. These are people who can make you a better lawyer and help you understand different industries and the problems that your clients might face.

2. Podcasting Is a Way to Deepen My Relationships with Other Professionals and Grow My Network

When I meet professionals who serve some of the same clients, inviting them to be on *Counsel to Counsel* is a way to get to know them better and a way to build our relationship. Spending time interviewing other professionals helps me understand ways that I can be of help to them and that they can be of help to me. It is also a way to stay on people's radar.

While the medium has been around for more than a decade, most people that I invite still think of it as a novel way for them to get exposure. If I meet someone through ProVisors (my business networking group) or through any other professional or personal activity, the first step in getting to know them might be to invite them to coffee (in person or virtual). During that conversation, if it seems like they could be a good guest (i.e., because they have something to teach me that might be of interest to my audience), I ask if they would be willing to be interviewed.

I explain that there is very little preparation and that they can use it as marketing collateral for their own business (e.g., if they need to market for their work). Most people I speak to say yes. This gives me a chance to speak to them a third time (I usually book the interviews a month or two after our coffee—sometimes more).

You can also deepen your relationship with your clients by inviting them on as guests.

3. Podcast Interviews Are Resources That I Can Share with My Clients

Now that I have been producing *Counsel to Counsel* for six years, I have a good library of resources that I can share with my coaching clients. If I am working with an attorney on increasing his or her marketing visibility, I might share an interview I've done about social media or other types of legal marketing. If a client is thinking about an in-house career, I share several interviews I've done with in-house counsel. In short, I have resources to share with my clients, particularly "evergreen content" that doesn't go stale.

Professional writing can serve some of the same purpose. Matt Yospin, a solo IP lawyer in the Boston area, has done a great job of creating written content that he shares when he gets inquiries about trademark, copyright, and other generic IP issues. It saves him a lot of time in responding to the many inquiries he gets (many from people who will never become clients).

But everyone has different preferences. Podcasts are portable, and you can listen to them while commuting, chopping vegetables for dinner, or taking a walk. So having a library of articles and podcast episodes is a way for you to quickly educate your clients on a subject (or answer common questions you get from your clients).

4. Podcasts Can Be a Lead-Generation Tool

Putting a podcast out into the world is also a way to generate some leads for my coaching business. Over the last several years, I've had a number of lawyers tell me during an initial consultation that they have listened to a number of episodes and that is why they reached out. But it is not a tool that generates a lot of leads, so I've listed this last.

One reason why podcasts help with lead generation is that hearing your voice creates more familiarity. People feel like they have a better sense of who you are when they hear you speaking rather than just reading what you have written. People hire lawyers whom they know, like, and trust. Hearing your voice is a way to demonstrate that you are likable and trustworthy. (Video can also be very powerful in that way.)

Podcasting has also generated leads for me because doing a regular podcast is a way for me to remind individuals in my network (particularly people I am connected to on LinkedIn) that I exist. Writing and speaking do this as well. But people subscribe to podcasts, so anyone who is a subscriber gets reminded twice a month about my services.

Finally, having a podcast provides me with marketing collateral to send to people after I have done a free consultation (i.e., I send them a link to an interview on a topic that relates to why they might want to work with a coach). This can help reinforce why I might be the right person to help them.

Miscellaneous Tips for Podcasting Success

Podcasting can be a pretty large time commitment. If you have more money than time, consider hiring a producer who can edit your interviews, create show notes, and help you promote the podcast once it has been released. Here are some other tips to help you be successful:

1. Launch a podcast only if you like interviewing people. There are many ways to market yourself. I always tell my clients to choose those activities that they enjoy (i.e., activities you enjoy that will help you build your reputation and referral relationships). Don't start a podcast just because you think you "should"!
2. Choose a niche that targets the clients or referral sources you want to reach. Most podcasts have relatively small audiences, but if you find the "right" community of listeners, you don't need a big following to get value. I know a corporate lawyer who several years ago created a podcast to interview owners of craft breweries. She actually got a new client after only three episodes.
3. Be consistent. The best podcasts are produced at regular intervals so that they can build their audience. I do *Counsel to Counsel* twice a month and release episodes on Sundays. While you don't have to commit to twice a month, once a quarter or randomly is not likely to be often enough to keep your audience engaged.
4. Podcasting is a medium that works best in short format. Aim to keep your episodes no more than 30 to 45 minutes long. Create a part 1 and a part 2 if you have a lot of content.
5. Figure out your voice and understand who you are trying to reach. I try to sprinkle humor into my podcasts, but I don't go overboard. I'm also not afraid to mix a little politics into my interviews. I figure anyone who appreciates my sense of humor or agrees with me politically is more likely to be a good client.

Podcasting has been a labor of love for me since 2018. In college, I really enjoyed anchoring the news on my campus radio station. But since that time (over 40 years ago), I had not been behind a microphone to do anything similar. Podcasting brought me back to that passion.

The internet has truly democratized the creation and dissemination of marketing content. It has never been easier to get your message out. But that also means that it has never been harder to break through the noise and reach the audience you want to reach (whether it is through phone calls, Zoom, email, publishing, public speaking, or now, podcasting).

So, think carefully about whether podcasting is for you. It could be that your time is better spent sitting on a nonprofit board, taking your contacts to sporting events, playing golf with them, or being active in a trade association.

But if you like learning, if you are looking for a way to deepen your relationships with professionals in your network, and if you enjoy interviewing people, give it a try. The barriers to entry are low, and you can see if it is right for you. As always, I welcome your inquiries to discuss.

USING AI TO GENERATE MARKETING IDEAS

I won't bury the lead. If you are not using AI for your marketing, you are missing a big opportunity to efficiently create marketing content. In chapter10, I demonstrated how I used ChatGPT to create a list of the types of information to collect about people in your network. In this chapter, I'm letting ChatGPT explain why you should use ChatGPT to support your content creation.

My prompt: *I coach lawyers on marketing. I want to write a short article on why my attorney clients should use ChatGPT to help them with their marketing. Please mention blog posts, LinkedIn posts, and summarizing articles the lawyer has read. Explain that ChatGPT does not substitute the lawyer's judgement, and the lawyer still has to review it for accuracy and tone.*

ChatGPT's response: *In the competitive legal industry, effective marketing can set an attorney apart from the rest. One tool that has proven invaluable for many of my clients is ChatGPT. Here's why every lawyer should consider integrating this AI into their marketing strategy.*

1. ***Crafting Blog Posts***
   Writing compelling and informative blog posts can be time-consuming. ChatGPT can help generate initial drafts based on topics you select. This allows you to focus on refining the content and ensuring it aligns with your expertise and style. The result is a polished blog post that showcases your knowledge and attracts potential clients.

(continued)

2. ***LinkedIn Posts***
   Maintaining a consistent presence on LinkedIn is crucial for networking and establishing thought leadership. ChatGPT can assist in creating engaging posts that highlight your achievements, share insights from recent cases, or comment on industry trends. This keeps your profile active and relevant, helping you to stay connected with your professional network.

3. ***Summarizing Articles***
   Lawyers often need to stay updated with the latest legal developments. ChatGPT can summarize lengthy articles, saving you time and providing a quick overview of key points. This can be particularly useful when sharing insights with colleagues or clients, ensuring they receive concise and clear information.

4. ***Enhancing Efficiency Without Replacing Judgment***
   It's important to note that while ChatGPT is a powerful tool, it does not replace your professional judgment. As an attorney, you must review and edit the content generated by ChatGPT to ensure it is accurate, relevant, and reflects your voice and tone. This collaborative approach combines the efficiency of AI with the expertise of a seasoned lawyer, resulting in high-quality marketing materials.

5. ***Conclusion***
   Incorporating ChatGPT into your marketing efforts can streamline your workflow and enhance your outreach. By leveraging this AI tool for drafting blog posts, creating LinkedIn content, and summarizing articles, you can focus more on what you do best: practicing law. Remember, ChatGPT is there to assist, but your professional insight is what ultimately makes the content truly impactful.

   Using ChatGPT wisely can give you a significant edge in marketing, helping you to reach and engage with a wider audience while maintaining the high standards of your profession.

CHAPTER 21
Do Rankings Matter?

If you are connected to any lawyers on LinkedIn, chances are, you've seen a lot of attorneys and law firms post about their Best Lawyers, Super Lawyers, or Chambers rankings. Maybe you are one of them.

If you want to promote your awards, do it tastefully.

- Don't make it all about you or start off with how "honored" or "humbled" you are.
- Make it about the teamwork and contributions of your colleagues.
- Focus on your clients, what you did this year workwise, or how you got to where you are today.
- Tell stories.

The threshold issue, though, is why you should post about this ***at all*** (and why I've made a concerted effort to let people know that I have won the Massachusetts Lawyers Weekly Reader Rankings Awards in three categories since 2021 (#1 or #2 in Lawyer Outplacement, Business Development Coach, and Executive Coaching).

RANKINGS ALONE DON'T GENERATE WORK, BUT THEY DO HAVE VALUE

It is easy to be a little cynical about rankings. After all, there is no panel of judges sitting around giving out these awards. Instead, the winners are generally the individuals and law firms who were the most effective in getting out the vote.

Furthermore, Best Lawyers, Super Lawyers, the Massachusetts Lawyers Weekly Reader Rankings Awards, and similar publication inside and outside the legal industry all generate significant advertising revenue (that is paid by the recipients of these awards to the publications that award them).

In addition, it is highly unlikely that any prospective client is going to call you just because you are a "Best Lawyer" or a "Super Lawyer."

In my case, I asked A LOT of people to vote for me for the *Massachusetts Lawyers Weekly* (*MLW*) Reader Rankings Awards. And you can be sure that not all of them were paying clients. As a result, I have been named a top coach since 2021 (in the categories of Business Development Coach, Lawyer Outplacement, and Executive Coaching). I have also spent real money to take advantage of the advertising programs that are offered by *MLW* (in 2022, it was the first time I had spent money on advertising in over 15 years!).

But I don't expect these ads to generate inquiries from lawyers who don't already know me.

So why invest any time, energy, and $ to participate in these rankings?

The short answer is that getting ranked is validating. If someone has been referred to you, they are going to Google your name and check out your on-line bio. Seeing on LinkedIn or on your law firm website that you've been ranked demonstrates that someone thinks you are good at what you do.

It's not why someone looks you up in the first place; but it provides something tangible to corroborate what the referral source said about you. Or if they learned about you when you did a presentation or published an article, seeing these added credentials in your bio is helpful.

Of course your bio should also be filled with representative matters that feature the types of clients you have worked with and the types of problems you solved for those clients.

CLIENTS HIRE LAWYERS WHO THEY KNOW, LIKE, AND TRUST

Most people who hire lawyers don't have a good way to evaluate their competence. Instead, clients are looking for proxies to prove that the attorney can do the work and provide quality legal representation.

If clients are given two names and only one of those lawyers has awards to his or her name, the other lawyer will be at a disadvantage. Displaying these awards helps to build trust.

Furthermore, asking people to vote for you is a way to continue to remind your clients, prospective clients, and referral sources that you are out there. Since legal services are by their nature high-end purchases that don't happen every day, finding ways to remain visible over time is key in building your practice.

Finally, announcing that you have been acknowledged is a great opportunity to thank your clients and referral sources. (And it's a chance for you to receive a lot of "attaboys." Don't underestimate how good it feels to have people congratulate you. I know it feels great when I make my own announcements.)

There are many ways to spend time and money to generate work. Rankings are certainly not the most important thing to focus on in your marketing arsenal.

But they shouldn't be ignored either.

Just don't let buying advertising in one of these publications be a substitute for genuine relationship building. Investing in relationship building is ultimately where you'll get the most bang for your buck.

CHAPTER 22

Marketing Lessons from the Oval Office

"Take government off the backs of the great people of this country." In 1980, Ronald Reagan spoke these words at a presidential debate with Jimmy Carter. He went on to a decisive win in that election, and in his first inaugural address he declared, "Government is not the solution to our problems; government is the problem."

While these messages never resonated with me (I've always leaned left of center), what I have come to realize is that Reagan really *was* the great communicator. More than almost any other president in US history, Reagan understood how to construct and deliver an effective marketing message.

I've also come to appreciate that regardless of what we think of the message or even of the messenger, we can learn a lot about selling legal services (good and bad) by observing the occupant in the oval office (and the candidates vying for that office). Here are some of these lessons.

KEEP IT SIMPLE, STUPID (THE KISS METHOD)

A lot can be said about Reagan's rhetorical style and why he was so successful in convincing the American public to turn on government. A significant key is that Reagan was able to simplify complexity and not get bogged down in the details. He understood that crafting a succinct slogan would do a lot more than communicating a complex message.

Contrast Reagan's message about government with President Joe Biden's messaging on the second infrastructure package (a package I completely supported). Build Back Better has to be one of the worst names ever crafted for a bold piece of legislation. And the bill itself was too complex for anyone to understand. In fact, while polling demonstrated that a majority of Americans supported the contents of the bill (including me, for the most part), no one actually knew what it contained. Eventually, Congress passed the Inflation Reduction Act of 2022, which incorporated some of the Build Back Better Act's climate change, healthcare, and tax reform proposals while excluding its social safety net proposals.

What is the legal marketing takeaway? When you are trying to market your practice, your message needs to be simple and memorable.

When someone asks what you do, don't list everything. Pick one, two, or maybe three problems you solve for clients. Say it in a way that is memorable.

Chris Murphy of Scalli Murphy Law in Everett, Massachusetts, introduces himself by saying: "Call me if you or someone you know is in the back of an ambulance or the back of a hearse." Saja Raoof, an immigration lawyer in San Francisco, calls herself a "border wall destroyer." Mark Hankin, an IP lawyer in Los Angeles, says, "I protect what you have in mind."

Contrast that with the general practitioner who does real estate closings, divorce, trusts and estates, OUI, corporate law, and bankruptcy. Or compare those taglines to the following description I saw on someone's LinkedIn profile:

> *I'm a transactional attorney concentrating in corporate, business, commercial lending, and finance law. I negotiate and close joint ventures, mergers and acquisitions (buyers and sellers), asset dispositions, securities issuances and other capital raises, recapitalizations, restructurings, buyouts and takeouts, as well as various types of business and real estate financing (ranging from venture and private equity to asset- and property-backed bank financing)....*

It actually goes on from there.

Keep in mind that a LinkedIn profile should be littered with keywords so that you can be found when someone does a search. In fact, this language could actually be part of an effective profile. But your headline, and certainly the first few sentences of your "About" section—and similarly your elevator pitch—should be short and sweet.

REPETITION IS EFFECTIVE

Another lesson we learn from presidents who succeed in winning the hearts and minds of their followers is that constant repetition can be very effective. If you take a simple message and repeat it over and over again, people will believe you. Trump's 2016 campaign slogan, "Make America Great Again," was easily repeatable (and sold a lot of hats). If you look at the winners of presidential elections throughout history, you'll see simple slogans repeated over and over. "Are you better off than you were four years ago?" (Reagan again). "Compassionate conservatism" (George W. Bush). "Hope and change we can believe in" (Barack Obama).

As lawyers, we are trained to be the smartest person in the room. But coming up with "new material" is not necessarily the best way to be remembered. Putting evergreen content on your website and speaking on basic topics in your field are more important than brilliance. (The only exception to this is when you are trying to hone a highly technical reputation and want to be known as the leading expert in your field.)

Trusts and estates lawyers, for example, can post articles on their website on why new parents need to have a will, set up a durable power of attorney, designate a healthcare proxy, etc. Employment attorneys can speak about how to effectively terminate an employee. Corporate lawyers can speak about traps to look out for when selling a business.

ALIGN YOURSELF WITH SUPPORTERS WHO WILL AMPLIFY YOUR MESSAGE

Presidents understand that in running for office and in selling a policy to the American public, they need supporters who will amplify their message.

As a lawyer in private practice, it is important to build strong relationships with referral sources who will tout your expertise and think of you when their clients have a need.

If a couple is in therapy and it becomes clear that divorce is inevitable, you want that therapist to give you a ringing endorsement when asked to recommend a good lawyer. If someone is talking to their accountant about getting investors for their business, you want that accountant to give that business owner your name as the "go-to" lawyer. If a parent in your kids' class is looking for a lawyer to prepare a will or represent them in a personal injury matter, you want the parents you know to recommend you (because they have seen you at PTA meetings, at drop-off, or on the soccer field).

SPEAK IN TERMS OF COMMON INTERESTS AND SHARED VALUES

Presidents know that finding communities with common interests and values is a great way to garner political support. Many Republican candidates since Reagan have courted the Christian right. But Barack Obama found out the hard way how that can backfire when he made his comment about people who "cling to their guns or religion" (a message that might have played well in liberal blue states but not so well in the heartland).

In building your network of clients and referral sources, look for people who share your interests and your values.

BE A GREAT LISTENER

Bill Clinton is the president who is probably best known for being a great listener. In the fictional account of his presidential run, *Primary Colors*, Clinton is described as someone with aerobic listening skills. He has the gift of making everyone, even everyone in a large room, feel as if he is really listening to them.

The single most important skill in developing your practice is being a great listener. By being a great listener, you will hear about the problems your clients, potential clients, and referral sources are trying to solve. You will be able to help them solve those problems either by referring them to a resource that can help or by providing your services to them or their clients.

HIRE GREAT MARKETING PROFESSIONALS

In the Bush versus Dukakis election, we saw how George H.W. Bush used a crackerjack marketing team to tar Michael Dukakis with the "Willie Horton" ad. Horton, a convicted murderer, committed assault, armed robbery, and rape while on furlough from prison under a program that was in place in Massachusetts while Dukakis was governor. During the same campaign cycle, Michael Dukakis appeared in a photo shoot sitting in an army tank, where he looked very silly and out of place. Clearly, Bush's campaign team led by Lee Atwater made the better choice (at least when viewed solely from the standpoint of effective marketing).

Just because you are a great lawyer that doesn't mean that you are great at advertising. With the rise of digital marketing and social media, there are a lot of choices to make and a lot to know. Choose marketing experts to help you.

CONCLUSION

I get great inspiration from watching how politicians get their messages across. While I find some of these messages truly outrageous, I know there is a lot to be learned.

If you want to get more legal work, follow the experts. There is no harder prize to win than getting elected to the office of president of the United States. Be a student of those who have succeeded and those who have failed. It will help advance your marketing success in ways that will make your career more fulfilling. And maybe you'll make your practice *great again*!

CHAPTER 23
Marketing Lessons from the Squash Court

Last year, I decided to sign up for some clinics at my squash club. I enjoy the sport and find it to be an amazing workout. But I'd like to get better.

For the uninitiated, squash is a racquet sport that is essentially played in a giant box. Because the ball bounces a lot less than a tennis ball, the game is very strategic. You can't simply overpower the other player.

Great squash players are constantly moving. It is a small space, and it is important to get out of your opponent's way. It is equally important to not sit back and admire your shots. While the court is relatively small, if you don't make an effort to position yourself, your chances of getting to the ball drop precipitously.

There is a lot I know about squash. And there is a lot I learned from the clinics. But as I told our coach, "I've learned so much from you Chris. I just can't do anything you've taught me." (Being in constant motion is not my normal biological tendency.)

The essential problem is that I am trying to break bad habits, and that takes time. I am trying to shift my focus on the squash court. And I need a lot of reminders.

To make a long story short, there is a gap between my knowledge and my execution. And coaching is helping. Coaching is making me aware of what I am not doing.

For lawyers trying to develop a practice, the issue is similar. Lawyers in private practice are trained to focus on the billable hour. It is hard to carve out time to call a referral source or make an effort to attend networking meetings if you have work on your desk.

The habit of monetizing your time is drilled into you from day one. And in the short term, there is no obvious reward for taking time out to write an article or go out to lunch with a past client.

There is also no clear immediate reward for being persistent. If you are like a typical lawyer, if a good referral source has not responded to your email inviting them to coffee, you are likely to think it is because of something you did (and trust me—that is usually my own default reaction).

But building a law practice does require persistence. Top rainmakers understand the great importance of consistency. Like in squash, you need to be moving all the time. And as in squash, positioning is important in marketing as well. You can't be everything to everyone or you'll be remembered by no one.

Coaching can help break your bad habits and set you on a path of doing all the small things that will lead to the big result. A good coach is a sounding board who helps you get past roadblocks, holds you accountable, and provides encouragement, which can help motivate you.

A good coach can create more urgency to do the things that you will be rewarded for in months or years.

Chris is going to have work harder to get me to stop staring at my feet. She is likely to be telling me the same five things for several more months. While I may never make it to the top of the tour (like her son Timmy, who is a national champion), with more time and $, I'm sure I'll start to incorporate what she has been trying to get me to do.

Put me in, coach!

CHAPTER 24
Marketing Lessons from Ted Lasso

It has been well over a year since I watched the final episode of *Ted Lasso*, and I still miss him! While it was sad to say goodbye to the wonderful characters in the show, I think a three-season run was just right for this one.

And like a good athlete, the "show" went out on top. (No spoilers—I won't say where AFC Richmond ended up at the end of their season.)

Ted Lasso, the heartwarming character from the hit TV show, offers several valuable marketing lessons that summarize much of what we've been discussing. As we get near the end of this book, I thought it would be useful to reflect on what we can learn from Ted about how to sell professional services!

- **Authenticity Matters:** Ted's genuine, kindhearted nature resonates with people. In marketing, authenticity builds trust and loyalty with your audience. See chapter 1.
- **Positivity and Optimism:** Ted's relentless optimism creates a positive environment. Positive messaging in marketing can inspire and attract customers. This is challenging for many lawyers but as we have been saying, it is helpful to put aside your pessimism when wearing your marketing hat. Even if you aren't feeling it, try to act more like an entrepreneur and see opportunity rather than risk.
- **Building Relationships:** Ted focuses on building strong, personal relationships with his team. Similarly, fostering strong relationships with potential clients and referral sources can lead to long-term loyalty.

- **Teamwork and Collaboration:** Ted emphasizes teamwork. In marketing, collaboration within your team and with your audience can lead to more innovative and successful campaigns. While we like our autonomy as lawyers, unless you are a sole practitioner, find ways to work with your partners to market together. Leverage your marketing team if you have one. Find ways to market with your referral sources through presentations and articles.
- **Preparation:** Like any good coach, Ted ensures that his team practices the skills that they will need during the game and comes to the game with a plan of action. Legal marketing requires planning and preparation as well. Don't try to wing it.
- **Adaptability and Resilience:** Ted faces numerous challenges but adapts and stays resilient. Marketing requires flexibility to adapt to changing trends and overcome setbacks. This is a big obstacle for many of us to get past. As we discussed in chapter 1, as lawyers, we don't like rejection. We don't like failure. Ted teaches us that it is important to learn from our failures (if they are mistakes), and to keep going (if failure is simply that the other team played a better game.)
- **Be a Goldfish:** When you make mistakes, shake them off and focus on the present. Ted taught us that a goldfish has a memory that lasts only five to ten seconds. If you want to optimize your performance, don't focus on what went wrong. Focus on what you are going to do next. If one networking meeting didn't go well, set up three more. If you sent a fee agreement to a new client and they are now ghosting you, focus on the two clients who did return the fee agreement.
- **Storytelling:** Ted's stories and anecdotes engage his team and make his messages memorable. Effective storytelling in marketing can captivate and retain your audience's attention. While Ted clearly had the gift for telling stories that seemed spontaneous and unrehearsed, for lawyers, it is important to craft good stories in advance.
- **Empathy and Understanding:** Ted's empathy helps him understand and connect with his team. Understanding your clients' needs and pain points can help tailor your marketing strategies to address them effectively.
- **Make People Feel Appreciated:** Ted is always striving to make members of the team feel appreciated. That included the players, the other coaches, and the business team. Make the people in your network feel appreciated and follow up with them over time. See chapter 18 for ideas about

appropriate ways to follow up with people in your network so that they know you care.

- **Engage in Small Acts of Kindness:** On his first day as the head coach of AFC Richmond, Ted started a tradition he called "Biscuits with the Boss." It was part of his effort to build a positive relationship with Rebecca, the owner of the team. Each day, Ted would present Rebecca with a small pink box of shortbread biscuits that he had baked himself. Despite her initial reluctance, Rebecca grew fond of the biscuits, and they became a symbol of Ted's persistence, kindness, and ability to win people over with small, thoughtful gestures. Your own small acts of kindness with clients, potential clients, and referral sources will pay off.
- **Humor Is a Great Tool for Breaking Down Walls:** Ted was a goofball. He came to the United Kingdom (UK) knowing nothing about soccer. But people came to trust him in part because he used humor to break down walls. See chapter 11 for more on the role of humor in strengthening connection.
- **Focus on the Long Game:** Ted looks at long-term growth and development rather than immediate wins. Sustainable marketing strategies that focus on long-term goals often yield better results than short-term tactics.

Ted Lasso is an American football coach who comes to the UK to coach an English soccer team. He knew nothing about the sport when he arrived. But he uses his strong sense of people to inspire the team to do their best. He is confident, and yet he displays a lot of humility.

As lawyers, we want to demonstrate strength to show our clients that we are competent and working hard for them. But we need to focus on human factors if we want to build a practice.

CHAPTER 25
Next Steps

"The more I learn, the more I realize how much I don't know."

—*Albert Einstein*

"CONSULTING: If you're not a part of the solution, there's good money to be made in prolonging the problem."

—*www.despair.com*

In the previous chapter, I talked about my favorite fictional coach and how he elevated the performance of a struggling soccer team in the UK. In this final chapter, I would like to explain why I believe that while training, podcasts, webinars, reading books like this, exercise, meditation, and therapy can all contribute to your success, coaching may be the missing link in elevating your own performance so you can achieve your marketing goals.

Not everyone needs to work with a coach. An increased understanding of what it takes to build a practice is enough for some lawyers to achieve marketing success. But working with a coach increases the odds and also speeds up the process.

I've worked with several coaches throughout my career, and I know that this has been the case for me. Attending many workshops on marketing and reading countless books and articles on the subject (and in the past ten years, listening to hundreds of podcasts) has dramatically increased my awareness of where to focus my energies. Coaching, however, is what has had the greatest impact on aligning my actions and mindset with my marketing goals.

TRAINING IS A VALUABLE FIRST STEP

Education is in my blood. My father was a math professor, and my mother was a school psychologist. I was also raised in an affluent Jewish suburb in New York where academic accomplishment was highly valued.

Earning a graduate degree was my destiny from a young age. And I still consider myself a lifelong learner. The content that is freely or cheaply available through podcasts, webinars, Google searches, social media, YouTube, traditional media sources, and now ChatGPT has only accelerated my learning.

Despite this, I realized early in my professional career that reading and classroom training will only get you so far. Webinars, books, articles, and other educational content can increase our awareness of things we didn't previously know. But changing our behavior takes more.

I had the good fortune of attending law school at Northeastern, which has a great co-op program. Before I graduated, I had worked for the US Attorney in Massachusetts, a plaintiff's toxic tort law firm, the public defender, and the Office of General Counsel at Boston University. I also participated in a clinical program at Northeastern called the Prisoners Assistance Project. These were great opportunities for experiential learning, and they taught me the value of hands-on education with active feedback.

When I finished law school in the late 1980s, my interest in the legal profession was still high. But as I noted in the Introduction, through my co-op jobs, I realized that my skills were best deployed in helping lawyers. Instead, I opted not to practice, and after graduation I joined Massachusetts Continuing Legal Education (MCLE) as a program attorney. Over the next seven years, I planned hundreds of CLE programs with leading attorneys, judges, and consultants. Many of these were panels of experts talking about both substantive law and more practice-oriented topics such as marketing and law firm management.

In a lot of ways, these seminars were simply an extension of law school classes but with a more practical bent. The material was often delivered in lecture format, and the panelists prepared course materials that included a lot of checklists, sample forms, and other practice tips.

These CLE programs provided (and still provide) an essential resource in filling in the gaps that we don't learn as lawyers in law school.

But during my time at MCLE, I realized that the most valuable courses we offered were the hands-on trial practice workshops where participants were essentially coached on their litigation skills.

BECOMING A SOLOPRENEUR

In the 1980s and 1990s, the new field of executive coaching was emerging. Corporations were beginning to deploy coaches for their executives not as a remedial measure but as a way to elevate performance.

Coaching was also just beginning to find its way into the legal profession, initially to help lawyers increase their marketing skills. Marketing was also relatively new for law firms. (The initial catalyst was the 1977 US Supreme Court case *Bates v. State Bar of Arizona*, 433 U.S. 350 [1977], in which the Court upheld the right of lawyers to advertise their services.)

When our second child was born, I realized that it was time to leave the nonprofit world. My job at MCLE was largely a recruiting job, so I decided to launch my own search firm. In 1997, Seckler Legal Consulting was born.

At the same time, I wanted to be more than just a recruiter. I had worked with a coach in setting up my own business, so I began offering both recruiting and coaching services to the legal community.

Within a few years, I began to truly appreciate the distinction between consulting and coaching, and eventually, I stopped using the word "consulting" in my business name. Today, I operate as Seckler Attorney Coaching, and I am no longer recruiting.

TRAINING IS AN ESSENTIAL FIRST STEP IN MAKING CHANGE; CONSULTING CAN FURTHER RAISE AWARENESS

At MCLE, I enjoyed getting to know some of the leading minds in the Massachusetts legal community. I watched how they navigated their careers, and I was truly impressed at how much time these successful lawyers were willing to volunteer to help younger lawyers learn the practical skills they needed to be successful.

I also had the chance to plan numerous seminars put on by some great consultants.

I particularly enjoyed organizing and attending the more practice-oriented courses. I helped create a course entitled "How to Make Money and Stay Out of Trouble," which is still going strong more than two decades later.

I also brought in some of the pioneers in legal marketing to "educate" lawyers about the marketing skills they didn't learn in law school. I, myself, became a "student" of all things marketing.

These seminars made me aware of what I needed to know in order to be successful in generating work. But it wasn't until I began implementing these ideas that I realized I needed help in getting my own business to the next level. Training didn't necessarily change my behavior. Hiring a coach did.

Lawyers are good consumers of training. We get through law school because we are academically inclined. We are accustomed to listening to experts and turning to consultants for answers.

Law firms hire consultants to set up accounting systems, IT, websites, and a host of other marketing functions. But when it comes to our own individual performance, there is a gap between knowing and doing.

Continuing legal education programs and other outside training can provide some of the solutions, and hiring consultants can also be a big help.

For most of us, however, attending some seminars, reading a few books, or bringing in an expert is not enough. Sergiu Simmel, a coaching colleague of mine, explained it this way: "You can't read the label from inside the jar." In other words, we all need a sounding board in order to change our behavior and achieve our goals.

HIRING A COACH IS LIKE HIRING A PERSONAL TRAINER

Coaching is for lawyers who want to elevate their performance, increase their career satisfaction, and acquire the missing nonlegal skills that are necessary for success. It is similar in many ways to personal training. You might hire a personal trainer to help you develop and follow a fitness plan. Although you may already have a good idea of how to get in shape, you may be uncertain about which exercises to do, how long to spend on each one, or how to use the equipment at the gym properly.

Along the way, the personal trainer helps you to develop short-term goals that support your long-term objectives. The trainer then holds you accountable. The trainer might support you when you are having difficulty and even suggest another approach when something is not working. Or the trainer might push you to the edge of your comfort zone.

That's why star athletes all have personal trainers.

Similarly, a lawyer hires a coach to help clarify professional goals and create an action plan for reaching these goals. Along the way, the coach provides support and serves as a sounding board and a resource. The coach also helps the attorney identify and move past roadblocks that are preventing success. A good coach then holds the lawyer accountable for achieving these goals. Hiring a coach creates the urgency to focus on those things that are important but not urgent. In a profession that is largely driven by billable hours, this sense of urgency about what is "important but not urgent" can make the difference between marketing action and inaction.

COACHING IS NOT THERAPY, BUT IT IS THERAPEUTIC

Therapy is a relationship designed to help individuals address emotional, psychological, or behavioral issues. Therapists work to heal past traumas, manage mental health issues, and improve overall well-being. They use their clinical expertise to help clients understand and work through their past and present struggles, often focusing on healing and emotional stability.

Unlike therapists, coaches typically don't give advice or heal past trauma. Instead, they help individuals harness their own strengths and potential, focusing primarily on the future.

I like to tell my clients, "I'm not a real doctor, I'm a juris doctor. But I play one on Zoom." I don't diagnose or heal mental health problems; but the work I do in helping my clients be more successful is helpful to their mental health.

In addition, the knowledge that my clients bring into the room about the mental health challenges they have uncovered in working with a therapist can impact the choices they make in working on their professional goals.

WHAT ISSUES ARE SUITABLE FOR ATTORNEY COACHING?

Attorneys can use a coach to work on a broad mix of professional issues at any stage of their career. Many attorneys choose to work on business development because selling is not a skill that comes naturally to many attorneys, and it is not a skill that is taught in law school.

In my coaching practice, I spend a lot of time helping lawyers overcome their resistance to selling and helping them to reframe legal marketing as an enjoyable activity that relies on building mutually beneficial professional and personal relationships.

I also work with lawyers who are new to leadership roles. The things that make us effective in representing our clients (e.g., our skepticism, aversion to risk, analytical thinking, competitiveness, sense of urgency, and preference for autonomy) can interfere when we are trying to inspire others and build a team.

In addition, some of my clients are trying to figure out a better career fit in or out of the law. They need support in setting new career goals and in figuring out what steps to take to achieve those new goals.

Regardless of what we are working on, many of my clients need help with follow-up, goal setting, and general communication skills.

There are a lot of resources available to lawyers who need help with these issues. There is a lot you can read on the web about legal careers, marketing, and leadership.

If you attend some training programs, read articles, listen to podcasts, or hire a consultant, you can get a better understanding of where the gaps are in your ability to generate work, run a law firm or corporate law department, or navigate a career transition. You may even learn some practical tips.

Coaching is what gets you from knowledge to action.

Put another way, coaching stands as the crucial "last mile" in the journey of professional development. While training equips you with knowledge and consulting provides tailored advice, it is coaching that bridges the gap between awareness and overcoming inertia. While other forms of professional support may illuminate the path, coaching ensures you navigate it effectively, turning potential into tangible progress.

WHY ATTORNEY COACHING?

Attorneys are good candidates for coaching because they are results oriented. As busy professionals, attorneys have difficulty focusing consistently on things that are important but not urgent. Billable work often becomes the only priority in a lawyer's day. Important activities such as administrative tasks, marketing, and giving feedback and mentoring to more junior attorneys, frequently get put off. Coaching helps create more urgency to focus on tasks that may not provide an immediate payback.

In addition, although attorneys may get good training in lawyering in the early years of practice, they are less likely to get guidance in developing a book of business.

As a coach, I will often help my clients to understand the big picture in what they are trying to accomplish. I have had many clients start talking to me about their website or LinkedIn profile before they have even established who is their ideal client. I recently had a client come to me for help with a resume. After we spoke for a while, I helped the client articulate that what she really needed help with was defining her career goals.

Attorneys are also good candidates for coaching because they score high on personality traits such as skepticism and autonomy and low on traits such as sociability. Because coaching is generally one-on-one and not a "one-size-fits-all" solution, coaching gives lawyers the chance to take the lead in finding their own solutions by working with a coach who asks in-depth, individualized questions. This helps them get past their own skepticism and not waste time on issues they don't find relevant. As one client of mine recently said, coaching provides a safe space to explore challenges without feeling "foolish."

WHEN SHOULD I HIRE A COACH?

There is no "right" time to hire a coach, but hiring a coach early on can avoid a lot of problems down the road.

Many attorneys hire a coach when they feel a pressing need. They want to make partner and need to learn how to develop a book of business. They want to go in-house but aren't sure how to conduct a job search. They were elevated to chair of a practice group and are used to being an individual contributor rather than a leader. They want to start their own firm.

Some lawyers may be stuck in a practice area that is not satisfying.

A coach can help a lawyer identify problem areas, create an action plan, and follow through.

CALMING THE NEGATIVE CHATTER IN YOUR HEAD

In my opinion, one of the greatest barriers to our marketing success is negative self-talk. A coach can help with this as well. But hiring a coach is not the only way to get past your self-limiting beliefs that are interfering with your success.

If you are like me, the internal voices of doubt will never entirely disappear; however, you *can* learn to ignore or manage your inner dialogue and act in a way that will help you reach your goals. It is also likely that as you rack up some marketing successes, your tendency to think like a lawyer will diminish. Your brain will rewire to some extent.

One great technique for taking charge of your inner critic is to practice mindfulness meditation. Try out one of the many mindfulness meditation apps on your phone. I use Ten Percent Happier (see footnote 1 in chapter 4 for more suggestions—note that the app was recently named Happier). Yoga is also popular. Even the simple act of focusing on your breath a few times a day can improve your focus or calm your nerves (e.g., before you walk into a networking event, give a presentation, or meet an important client for coffee).

Exercise in general is a good way to calm the mind and reduce the negativity that is interfering with taking action.

Another technique that I use for calming my chatter is to go back and review nice letters and testimonials that I have received from clients. Having a client tell me "I'm so glad to have you by my side" was very reaffirming.

Many of your friends in private practice are likely dealing with the same issues. They are equally thrown off when they experience the same feelings of rejection that come up in selling any professional service. Showing some vulnerability with these friends is a way of normalizing your feelings and understanding that not every marketing activity will produce positive results.

I regularly check in with my coaching friends when I'm feeling that a prospect or a referral source is not being responsive. That helps me regain perspective and recognize that there are probably 20 reasons why they haven't replied to my three email messages—and none of them have to do with me.

Recently, I discovered a great method for dealing with the analysis paralysis that comes from playing back the negative tapes in my head. The technique is a way to decrease rumination by doing some self-talk in the second person. It is sometimes referred to as distanced self-talk. You can learn more about that on *Hidden Brain* podcast.[1]

In addition, practice self-compassion. Your lawyer's brain may think that self-compassion is self-indulgent. However, mindfulness practice teaches that self-compassion actually enhances empathy for others and strengthens relationships.

Calming the chatter in your head takes a lot of work. Over time, you can learn to take more control over your self-limiting beliefs. But waiting until your mindset shift is not a necessary prerequisite to start acting like an entrepreneur. Just focus on taking the first step and in all likelihood, inertia will carry you forward.

Finally, if you are truly feeling stuck, working with a coach is great way to address these issues. A good coach can help you to see the patterns in your behavior and thinking and help you act in a way that is more consistent with achieving your goals. Coaching is a way to ensure that your inner voice doesn't derail your success. Coaching can help you manage the voice that wants you to avoid risk and rejection. Sometimes, just the positive encouragement from a coach is enough to help you change your behavior.

[1] For a great discussion of rumination and how to tamp it down, listen to "Befriending Your Inner Voice," an episode of *Hidden Brain* podcast from 2022.

HOW DO I CHOOSE A COACH?

Hiring a coach is a very personal decision. Many coaches will give you a free consultation or coaching session. This provides you with the opportunity to see if you have good chemistry with that individual. Beyond chemistry, there are some objective considerations.

The more specialized your need may be, the more you should expect to pay. For example, a coach who can help with improving your general delegation skills would probably cost less than a coach who has deep subject-matter knowledge about how to set strategic direction for a midsized law firm or how to market a niche legal practice.

There are a range of styles in coaching, and you should decide which style best suits your personality. Do you want someone who will "hold your feet to the fire"? Do you want someone who will give you a lot of positive feedback? Do you prefer to work with someone who is very structured or someone who is flexible?

My style tends to be more flexible and encouraging. Because I have been in the legal profession for more than 30 years and I've worked with lawyers in every conceivable type of role, I bring my "consulting" hat to my coaching work.

The bottom line is to find someone you feel you can work with and trust. Often, this will mean finding someone who has been referred to you by someone else you trust.

WHO ARE COACHES?

At present, coaching still remains a relatively unregulated profession. Professionals come to coaching with a wide range of backgrounds. Lawyers often work with experienced members of the bar who have been through their own process and want to share what they have learned.

Coaches may also have a background in marketing, business, psychology, or career counseling, and some have been through a certification program offered by the International Coaching Federation.

While I've never taken the time to get certified formally as a coach, I've been working with my own coaches on and off for more than 25 years. I've attended countless trainings, read hundreds of articles and books, listen regularly to podcasts, and I consult monthly with a peer group of coaches who hold me accountable and help me elevate my own performance as a coach.

ARE YOU READY FOR COACHING?

Practicing law can become a vicious cycle of constantly trying to bill more hours and saving everything else for a rainy day. Real career satisfaction takes both hard work and planning. This shouldn't wait for a rainy day.

Many lawyers do not take the time to reflect on what they really want. Some do not know what steps to take to achieve their goals. Others know the steps but cannot get themselves to take action.

In my experience, attorneys who build their own practice, figure out what they really enjoy doing, and develop the soft skills that are not emphasized in the practice of law are happier attorneys.

WHO SHOULDN'T HIRE A COACH?

Most lawyers can benefit from the accountability that comes with coaching. But lawyers who are not committed to changing their behavior, lawyers who are not open to feedback, lawyers who are not willing to invest time between coaching sessions to do the work that is necessary, and lawyers who have a fixed mindset about their capabilities (e.g., "I'm not good at marketing) will probably not get a lot of benefit from hiring a coach.

A coach can't lift the weights for you (or reach out to your ten best contacts for coffee).

As we discussed earlier in the book, we have a strong need to demonstrate how smart we are, and asking for help means showing some vulnerability. If you are unwilling to receive help from another professional and you think you should be able to go it alone, you may not be a good candidate for coaching. Lawyers are not always good at seeking out help. If you see yourself as a problem solver and believe you can solve all of your own problems, then coaching is "unnecessary."

Sometimes, a firm will pay for an individual lawyer to receive coaching. The lawyer should accept this benefit only if he or she is prepared to do the work. Coaching is about making change. It works only if the lawyer is willing to put in the effort.

As a practicing lawyer, you may be able to solve your client's problems and see with clarity where they are getting stuck. That doesn't mean you can do this for yourself. A good coach can help you see what you are unable to see in yourself and get you "there" quicker.

So, what are you waiting for?

Closing Thoughts

I have spent most of my adult life trying to stop thinking like a lawyer. With this book, I'm finally throwing in the towel and saying to myself "I can be successful without changing my default wiring." As long as I'm willing to act like an entrepreneur, I will achieve the success I want.

Maybe my wiring has changed somewhat. I'm sure it has. But I continue to go through life with a recurring fear rejection, a healthy dose of skepticism, and a tendency to overanalyze everything. There is also a part of me that still feels uncomfortable with selling.

At the same time, I'm finally able to say unequivocally that I am an excellent coach, I provide a lot of help to lawyers, my services are valuable, and it is fine to proclaim that.

My father's voice (businesspeople are all "operators") and my mother's anxiety (the world is a dangerous place so be cautious) still haunt me. But they won't stop me from taking chances.

My message to you is that if you are committed to changing your behavior, you can learn to ignore the self-sabotaging voices in your head that play an important role in making you a great lawyer but hinder your ability to build a great practice.

Writing this book was a way of proving to myself that I am able to engage in self-promotion in a way that feels authentic to me. I have proven to myself that I can have one big negative thought (*Do I really have anything original to say?*) and write a book anyway because I believe I have something worth sharing, a different way to say it, and writing a book is good for my business.

My hope is that in some small way, what I have written will give you a few tools to help you change your own behavior and enable you to achieve the marketing success you deserve. Don't stop thinking like a lawyer. Your clients need your legal mind to protect them and manage risk.

But if you want to build a successful practice, start acting like an entrepreneur. Set aside your skepticism and try some new things. Take some risks. Your career satisfaction will soar. All you need is a willingness to try.

To sum it all up, I'll quote my son's first-grade teacher (circa 2001): *If you think you can, you might. If you think you can't, you're right.*

Index